The Unbr⚫ken Circle

A Toolkit for Congregations Around Illness, End of Life and Grief

James L. Brooks, M.Div.

MARCH 2009

Developed with support from
the U.S. Cancer Pain Relief Committee and
the Griggs Family Foundation, LLC

Give Us Your Feedback

Let us know if you like this book.
How have you used the information?
Would you like additional information on these topics?
Visit www.iceol.duke.edu to provide feedback and to sign up
for updates from the Duke Institute on Care at the End of Life.

Duke Institute on Care at the End of Life
Duke University Divinity School
2 Chapel Drive
Durham, North Carolina 27708
919-660-3553
www.iceol.duke.edu

The Duke Institute on Care at the End of Life (ICEOL) and the
National Hospice and Palliative Care Organization (NHPCO)
are committed to helping faith communities and hospices
come together to care for people with serious illnesses and
their families. *The Unbroken Circle* was created by ICEOL and
developed as a companion resource to NHPCO's Caring
Connections program's *It's About How You Live—In Faith:
Community Outreach Guide*, a tool designed for hospices
interested in working with faith communities. To learn more,
go to www.caringinfo.org.

ISBN 0-9796790-1-X
© Duke Institute on Care at the End of Life

*The Unbroken Circle: A Toolkit for Congregations
Around Illness, End of Life and Grief*
was designed by Spring Davis
One-of-a-Kind Design, Durham, North Carolina

James L. Brooks, M.Div.

Reverend James L. Brooks is the executive director of Project Compassion in Chapel Hill, North Carolina, and the director of leadership training for the National Support Team Network. He is the author of *It's About How You Live– In Faith: Community Outreach Guide*, published by the National Hospice and Palliative Care Organization. Brooks was profiled as one of five "Emerging Leaders" nationally in State Initiatives in End of Life Care by the Robert Wood Johnson Foundation. He has served as a clinical manager for Big Bend Hospice in Tallahassee, Florida, and a program director for Eastern Area Community Ministries in Louisville, Kentucky. He holds an undergraduate degree from Wake Forest University, a Master of Divinity degree from The Southern Baptist Theological Seminary and is ordained in the United Church of Christ.

Duke Institute on Care at the End of Life

The Duke Institute on Care at the End of Life, based at Duke Divinity School in Durham, North Carolina, works to improve the care of seriously ill patients and their families by creating knowledge and rediscovering old wisdoms about the spiritual dimension of end of life care. For more information, go to www.iceol.duke.edu.

DUKE INSTITUTE ON CARE AT THE END OF **LIFE**

Caring Connections

Caring Connections, a program of the National Hospice and Palliative Care Organization (NHPCO), is a national consumer and community engagement initiative to improve care at the end of life. Supported by a grant from the Robert Wood Johnson Foundation, it offers free consumer and community outreach resources at www.caringinfo.org.

Caring Connections
a program of the
National Hospice and Palliative Care Organization

Project Compassion

Project Compassion, a nonprofit organization, creates community and provides support for people living with serious illness, caregiving, end of life and grief. Based in Chapel Hill, North Carolina, it helps faith communities, other organizations and individuals create caregiving support teams and offers related workshops and resources. Project Compassion's work has been recognized by the Robert Wood Johnson Foundation, the National Hospice and Palliative Care Organization, AARP, the National Council on Aging and the Lance Armstrong Foundation. To learn more, go to www.project-compassion.org.

Creating Community, Providing Support
PROJECT COMPASSION

About the Cover

The photograph on the front cover brings together people of different ages and diverse backgrounds to represent a powerful unbroken circle of care.

Thanks to the following hands: Ann Atwater, Chris Brady, James Brooks, Harold Dunlap, Jean Dunlap, Susan Dunlap, Anna Kasibhatla, Prasad Kasibhatla, Sonia Norris, Uma Scharf and Elaine Wilder.

The cover was photographed by Les Todd of Duke Photography in Goodson Chapel of the Duke Divinity School on the Duke University campus in Durham. The book, including the cover, was designed by Spring Davis.

Call to Action   1

The Crisis Response Approach   2
A Call to Faith Communities   3
Faith Communities as Circles of Care   4
Becoming Unbroken Circles of Care   5
Unbroken Circle v. Crisis Response   6
How This Toolkit Can Help   6

Creating Unbroken Circles of Care   9

Envisioning an Unbroken Circle   10
Supporting Others During Specific Seasons of Life   11
Getting Started   12
Creating Action Plans   14
Providing Leadership Development   18
Providing Education for the Congregation   19
Providing Congregational Care and Support   22
Providing Support Through Worship   26
Providing Effective Communication   28
Providing Supportive and Accessible Space   30

Support During Serious Illness   33

How This Toolkit Can Help   34
Changing Views of Illness   34
Illness as a Season of Life   35
Understanding Illness   35
The Impacts of Illness   36
Illness and Suffering   38
The Opportunities of Illness   38
Living With Caregiving   41
Creating Unbroken Circles Around Illness   43
Congregational Care   48
Caring for Children and Teens   55
Meeting the Needs of Ill People Through Worship   57

Support During the End of Life

How This Toolkit Can Help   62
Understanding Death and Dying   62
Death of a Child   66
Care at the End of Life   67
Preparing for the End of Life   69
Advance Care Planning   70
How Faith Communities Can Help   75
Congregational Action Planning   75
End of Life Education   76
Congregational Care   80
Incorporating End of Life Into Worship   86

Support Through Grief

The Uniqueness of Grief   90
The Purpose of Grief and Mourning   91
Reactions to Grief   92
Traumatic Grief   95
Children, Teens and Grief   95
Congregational Action Planning   96
Grief Education   97
Congregational Care   101
Support Following Traumatic Death   112
Incorporating Grief Into Worship   115

Glossary of Faith Community Terms

The Unbroken Circle was created by the Duke Institute on Care at the End of Life, thanks to the work of many passionate people who believe that congregations are a vibrant place to address issues of advanced illness, dying and grief. We are deeply grateful to all those who so willingly gave their time and talent in writing, researching, reviewing, editing, designing and funding it.

The Production Team:

The Reverend James L. Brooks, MDiv, *Author*	Project Compassion
Lindley Sharp Curtis, MSW, MDiv, *Contributor*	Duke Divinity School
Merry Davis, *Production Manager*	Duke Institute on Care at the End of Life
Spring Davis, *Graphic Designer*	One-of-a-Kind Design
Meridith M. Grandy, *Researcher*	Duke Divinity School
Dana Hall, *Administrative Assistant*	Duke Institute on Care at the End of Life
Sonia Norris, *Researcher*	Project Compassion
Barbara Kate Repa, *Editor* and *Production Manager*	Independent Consultant
Jeanne S. Twohig, *Project Manager*	Duke Institute on Care at the End of Life

Advisors:

Tonya D. Armstrong, PhD, MTS	Duke Divinity School
Alyson J. Breisch, MSN, RN, FCN	Duke Divinity School
The Reverend Lamar J. Brooks, DMin, MDiv	Baptist Pastor, Retired
Mary Margaret Brooks, MDiv	North American Mission Board
Carolyn H. Burrus, MDiv	Hospice of Alamance-Caswell
Bishop Kenneth L. Carder	Duke Divinity School
John C. Dormois, MD	John C. Dormois, M.D., LLC
The Reverend Susan J. Dunlap, PhD	Duke Divinity School
Elizabeth Eder, MDiv	Duke Divinity School
Margaret H. Frothingham, RN, MCM	Blacknall Memorial Presbyterian Church
Paul J. Griffiths	Duke Divinity School
Artie Hendricks, MDiv, ThM	Duke University Medical Center
Joan Mellen, RN	John C. Dormois, M.D., LLC
Anne A. Packett, MA, RN, FCN	Duke Divinity School
Richard Payne, MD	Duke Institute on Care at the End of Life
The Reverend Tarris Rosell, PhD, DMin	Center for Practical Bioethics
Jodi Simmons, MDiv, BCC	Duke Home Care and Hospice
The Reverend Bill Simons	United Methodist Church, North Alabama Conference
Gwynn Sullivan, RN, MSN	National Hospice and Palliative Care Organization
Allen Verhey, PhD	Duke Divinity School
The Reverend Patty Walker, MDiv	Pikes Peak Hospice
The Reverend Donald J. Welch, DMin	Seven Lakes Chapel in the Pines
The Reverend Jack B. Yarbrough	Centenary United Methodist Church

And special thanks to our funders:

Griggs Family Foundation, LLC

United States Cancer Pain Relief Committee

And to our organizational partners:

National Hospice and Palliative Care Organization/ Caring Connections

Project Compassion

A Call to Action

The Crisis Response Approach 2

A Call to Faith Communities 3

Faith Communities as Circles of Care 4

Becoming Unbroken Circles of Care 5

Unbroken Circle v. Crisis Response 6

How This Toolkit Can Help 6

For everything there is a season
and a time for every matter under heaven:

A time to be born and a time to die

A time to plant and a time to pluck up what is planted;

A time to kill and a time to heal ...

A time to weep and a time to laugh;

A time to mourn and a time to dance ...

A time to embrace and a time to refrain from embracing;

A time to seek and a time to lose;

A time to keep, and a time to throw away;

A time to tear, and a time to sew;

A time to keep silence, and a time to speak;

A time to love, and a time to hate;

A time for war, and a time for peace.

ECCLESIASTES 3:1-8

To provide feedback
on this toolkit, go to
www.iceol.duke.edu.

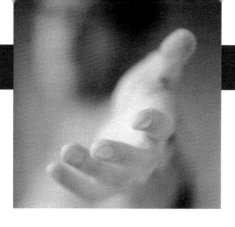

People facing illness, caregiving, end of life and grief often turn to their faith communities for support, seeking help with the spiritual, emotional and practical challenges these experiences bring. However, most congregations do not have the resources, training and support they need to offer comprehensive caring ministries for people during these important times.

All congregations are significantly affected by illness and caregiving, end of life and grief. During any given year, some members will be diagnosed with a serious or life-threatening illness. Others will see the health of people they love deteriorate. Some will receive an unexpected phone call with news of a shocking death. Many members will experience profound grief.

Realistically understood, illness, end of life and grief are important seasons of life that affect everyone at some point. These seasons may extend for months or years— sometimes decades—affecting every aspect of all those involved. As communities of faith, it is important to anticipate these seasons and to help members prepare for and weather them.

One of the challenges faith community leaders face is knowing how to help their congregations respond to the range of needs people experience as they cope with these difficult life passages. Many leaders

Within the circles of our lives we dance the circles of the years, the circles of the seasons within the circles of the years...

Wendell Berry,
American Author

already feel that they lack the time, staff, expertise and lay support to meet the many competing demands they face. In addition, clergy and lay leaders may not be sufficiently informed about the issues involved. And members may be afraid to address them.

The Crisis Response Approach

When offering support, many congregations rely on a crisis-response approach. Following a diagnosis, accident, surgery or death, congregations often mobilize to provide meals, visits, calls, cards, prayer and other support. Typically this significant attention lasts for days or sometimes weeks, but then much of the support often wanes.

As the people affected are discharged from the hospital to go home, move into a nursing facility or begin to cope with grief, their lives have changed. While their needs may be diminished following the crisis, new needs for support emerge. It then becomes difficult, if not impossible, for congregations that are invested in a crisis response approach to sustain effective spiritual, emotional, practical and social support for community members. As a result, the needs of many individuals and families go unmet in the weeks, months or years that follow the crisis.

The crisis response approach assumes it is out of the norm for people to deal with illness, dying or grief for extended periods. But this is

out of synch with reality. In fact, 90% of Americans will live with a serious illness for a year or more during their lifetimes. The question for most is not "if" they will face a long-term illness, it's "when?"

A crisis response model also assumes that needs will not increase. However, the country's changing demographics tell a very different story. While children, teens and adults of all ages can experience life-threatening illness or sudden death, two-thirds of people who are affected each year are seniors. And the number of seniors is expected to nearly double in the next 25 years as the Baby Boom generation ages. Life expectancy is increasing. People age 85 and older currently make up the fastest growing segment of the population, and a sizeable group of those older than 100 is emerging. The number of people suffering from chronic illness and functional disability will increase as more people live longer.

Even if faith communities were to double their staff and double their lay leadership, doing "more of the same" crisis response will not meet the deep and abiding long-term needs members face today. More importantly, the model will not begin to address the demographic changes that are quickly approaching. The crisis-response mode does not fully account for the kind of support people need through the seasons of illness, end of life and grief. And as time goes on, the crisis response approach will be less and less a viable option for faith communities.

A Call to Faith Communities

The time has come for faith communities to reassess their approaches to helping members experiencing illness, end of life and grief by asking:

- What can we do to ensure that all people will remain connected with their faith community throughout these important seasons of life?

- How can we mobilize care and support for people living with illness, end of life and grief?

- How can we become a supportive community for all people during these challenging times through our education, congregational care, worship, communications and accessible facilities?

At the heart of these questions is also a call to revisit what it means to be community. One definition identifies four key elements--all of them essential for nurturing a sense of community.

Membership: The feeling of belonging or of sharing a sense of personal relatedness.

Influence: A sense of mattering—of an individual making a difference to a group and of the group mattering to its members.

Integration and fulfillment of needs: The feeling that individual needs will be met by the resources received through membership in the group.

Shared emotional connection: The commitment and belief that members have shared and will share history, places, experiences and time.

Consider what happens when illness, end of life or grief makes it difficult for members to be actively involved in the faith community. While such people may maintain their memberships and may continue to feel the influence of the community, they are less and less integrated into it. Often their new needs are not met consistently. The emotional connection they may have experienced in the past diminishes as they have less energy and fewer opportunities to share their stories, experiences, challenges and spiritual growth with others.

The loss of community can feel even more profound following a faith community crisis response. When faith communities respond during a crisis period, people can experience strong, even overwhelming support. This leads them to believe that the faith community will be there for them as they need it. Then when the crisis subsides and the support wanes or disappears entirely, their sense of community is weakened even more.

But when congregations are able to offer a strong sense of community, individual members are not the only ones to benefit. By seeking new ways to reach out and incorporate people living with illness, end of life and grief into congregational life, faith communities open themselves to the insights these challenges bring—and gain the opportunity to learn from people going through them.

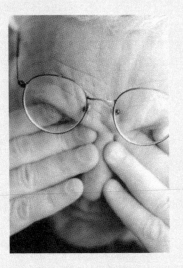

Dealing With Serious Illness

William and Dorothy had been active in their faith community for many years. They were married there, raised children there and stayed involved after they retired. Late one night, William felt sharp pains in his chest—the first signs of a massive heart attack. Dorothy called 911. Both of their lives changed overnight.

The days that followed felt like weeks to them, filled with hospitalizations, surgeries, sleepless nights, difficult decisions. At first, friends and faith community members visited, brought food, called and wrote cards. But as weeks turned into months, that support waned. Left alone to cope with William's illness, Dorothy felt worn out. She wondered how long she could go on.

Facing the End of Life

When Andrea was diagnosed with cancer three years ago, she moved in with her sister Lenora for support. Andrea was devastated a few months ago when it became clear that the cancer was no longer responding to treatment.

The burden of illness and caregiving had been so great for so long, Andrea and Lenora had not stayed connected with their faith community. At the same time, their congregation lost touch with them. Now that Andrea was dying, she and Lenora missed their faith community even more, and longed to be a part of it.

Faith Communities as Circles of Care

To fully understand what faith communities could offer members during illness, end of life and grief, consider the ways they support people at the beginning of life.

When a baby is born into a faith community, there is cause for celebration. Many faith traditions incorporate a ritual or sacrament for the baby and family members into worship: a baptism, a baby or parent dedication, a naming ceremony, a brit milah. While faith traditions interpret these rituals differently, they all connect the newborn and family in some way with God, with one another and with the community of faith. These rituals usually include the community's promise to take an active role in the newborn's life, to support him or her as a child of the faith.

Faith communities often shape themselves around this promise. They integrate care and support for children into every aspect of congregational life by providing:

- nurseries so that parents can attend worship and children can become accustomed to being part of a faith community

- worship services designed especially for them

- education to help them learn the stories, beliefs and traditions of the faith

- education for their parents who seek to raise them in the faith, and

- social opportunities for them to learn and grow together.

Through rites of passage such as confirmation, bar mitzvah or bat mitzvah, and others, faith communities mark a child's transition into adulthood or full membership in the faith.

This comprehensive approach to care and support for children and teens flows from the faith community's commitment to the newborn and family.

For many members, this is the beginning of the circle of care.

Caring for New Faith Community Members

Not everyone, of course, is born into a faith community or tradition. Many people join as adults, through conversion, "believer's baptism," transfer of membership or other means.

However, faith communities often develop a thoughtful model for the beginning of membership that resonates with their model at the beginning of life. They offer rites of passage in worship, educational programs to nurture them in the faith, opportunities for ministry, outreach and social connection that integrate them into the community and support them spiritually.

Just as they do for newborns at the beginning of life, congregations promise a community of faith for new members.

This becomes the beginning of the circle of care for new faith community members.

Staying connected

As members move through adulthood or become established in the congregation, faith communities often use similar strategies to keep them involved. Many have created comprehensive, customized programs to engage young adults, married adults, single adults and seniors. Members can take part in worship, continue their education, provide hospitality, offer care and support for others, do outreach and social ministry, make music or art, teach and lead others. As long as people take the initiative to become involved in the life of the community, the congregation will be there for them.

For active members, this is the continuation of the circle of care.

However, no matter how active a

person has been, there often comes a moment in life when he or she can no longer remain active in the faith community because of serious illness, caregiving or grief. This change can develop slowly over months or years; it can happen in the blink of an eye. When it comes, it can radically alter the member's relationship with the faith community. For many people, it is the moment when the circle of community is most fragile.

For many people, this is the moment when the circle of care is most likely to be broken.

The challenge our congregation faces in the next 20 years is learning how to move from being a "come to" congregation into being a "go to" congregation.

Fred Morgan, *Senior Pastor, Hope Presbyterian Church, Austin, Texas*

Becoming Unbroken Circles of Care

Consider how congregational life would change if faith communities applied the same strategies they use for people at the beginning of their lives to those at the end of their lives.

Imagine if faith communities reached out to members facing illness, end of life and grief and took the initiative to:

- prepare them for the physical, emotional, spiritual and social matters they face, anticipating the kinds of support they need

- use an integrated approach to extending community to them—including worship, education, congregational care, hospitality and a favorable environment of care

- develop effective leadership structures, comprehensive new programs and resources to ensure that they are supported

- become creative in their approaches—using music, the arts and unexpected strategies to engage them and keep them connected, and

- provide support consistently over time.

Working Through Grief

When Jonathan died suddenly, his wife Heather became numb. She could not believe he had died. Members of Heather's congregation surrounded her and her two children during the funeral and right after it. They brought so much food that Heather was relieved when a neighbor offered to help store some of it in her large freezer.

Five months after Jonathan's death, Heather's waves of loneliness, anger and disbelief grew more intense. She had trouble concentrating at work and was often weepy. Her ten year-old son got into fights at school and her seven year-old daughter had frequent stomachaches and headaches.

When Heather made it to worship services, she found it hard to sit among the congregation without being overwhelmed with emotion. Some people didn't know what to say to her. Others said only: "Call me if there's anything I can do." Heather began to wonder whether what she was experiencing was normal—and whether she would ever feel at home in the congregation again.

Imagine what would happen if congregations began to fulfill the promise of community made to newborns and new members: There would be an unbroken circle that fully honors and supports each member from birth through death.

Unbroken Circle v. Crisis Response

While faith communities will always face urgent and unexpected situations, the hallmark of an unbroken circle is that illness, end of life and grief are fully expected. Preparation through education, worship, congregational care and hospitality will begin long before a diagnosis, hospitalization or death.

When this season of life does arrive, faith communities will anticipate that there will be weeks, months or years when individuals and families live day to day with the realities of illness and grief. These periods will be punctuated by times of critical transitions. No longer defined as "crises," critical transitions will be anticipated and faith communities will offer effective and ongoing support through them.

This unbroken circle approach will ensure that faith community members' sense of community will be fully sustained throughout illness, during the end of life and during grief. They will continue to be integrated into community life consistently. Their need for support will be fulfilled, and their shared emotional and spiritual connections will be sustained over time. Members will not be forced to cope alone because their faith community will have anticipated and prepared for the seasons of life ahead.

The time has come for faith communities across traditions to address this need for change.

How This Toolkit Can Help

The Unbroken Circle is a toolkit for professional clergy, faith community nurses and lay leaders who want to improve care and support for those facing serious illness, end of life and grief.

As mentioned, many people in the faith community who want to help feel overwhelmed by the range of needs involved, by competing demands of congregational life and by lack of knowledge or experience in dealing with these matters.

At the same time, there has been an explosion of resources on these topics, emanating from a wide range of disciplines, organizations and movements. Some come from the worlds of health care, social work, community organizing and psychotherapy. Others are offered by theologians, ethicists and chaplains. A few come from faith tradition offices and denominational organizations. But most clergy and

lay leaders do not have the time to locate, sift through and evaluate the tremendous flood of information now available.

Throughout this toolkit, you will have the opportunity to assess your congregation's capacity and access tools and resources to provide education, congregational care, worship, facilities and other ministries for people dealing with illness, end of life and grief.

Creating a vision for your faith community as an unbroken circle of care is more than just a good idea. Based on changing demographics, advancements in medical treatment and the fragmentation of families and communities, becoming an unbroken circle of care during illness, end of life and grief is fast becoming a top priority.

May you take bold new action to nurture this vision and create meaningful ministry and support for the whole people of God through all the seasons of life.

All rhythms of time beat in God's great heart: the time to be born and the time to die, the time to plant and the time to reap, the time to laugh and the time to weep.

All seasons of life are beautiful in their time, and provide occasion for God's great mercy.

James L. Brooks,
Executive Director, Project Compassion,
Chapel Hill, North Carolina

This toolkit provides
guidance for faith communities
facing overwhelming demands
and the thicket of existing resources by:

- helping congregations understand why
  improving care for people facing serious illness,
  end of life and grief is essential

- guiding faith community leaders and members
  in finding a new vision of what it means to be in
  community with people living with these challenges

- providing clergy, faith community nurses and lay
  leaders with selected resources to develop their
  knowledge and skills in these areas, and

- equipping faith community leaders with the practical
  guidance, tips, tools, examples and resources they need
  to develop innovative ministries around these issues.

A Resource for All Faith Traditions

While faith communities and traditions differ on end of life beliefs and practices, congregations are much more alike than different when it comes to creating community around people as they live with illness, end of life and grief.

Recognizing this, *The Unbroken Circle* includes program ideas, scripture, stories, quotes, poems and examples drawn from a wide range of faith communities and traditions. By drawing on many sources, it offers faith communities an opportunity to learn from each other as well as from the resources provided.

The concluding Glossary of Faith Community Terms defines the spiritual and religious language used in context of this toolkit. You may choose to adapt these terms to your individual setting.

Scripture references throughout this toolkit are taken from the New Revised Standard Version translation.

As a supplement to *The Unbroken Circle*, see the comprehensive annotated listing of belief statements, resolutions and resources developed by different faith traditions and denominations at **www.iceol.duke.edu**.

Envisioning an Unbroken Circle   10
    Leadership   10
    Education   10
    Congregational Care and Support   11
    Worship   11
    Communication   11
    Faith Community Space   11
Supporting Others During
Specific Seasons of Life   11
    Illness   11
    End of Life   11
    Grief   11
Getting Started   12
    Explore Your Own Experience   12
    Evaluate Your Congregational
    Trends   12
    Evaluate Your Congregation's
    Current Offerings   14
Creating Action Plans   14
Providing Leadership Development   18
    Assess Ideas and Resources   18
    Create a Leadership Action Plan   19
Providing Education for
the Congregation   19
    Evaluate Current Programming   19
    Plan Future Programming   20
    Create an Education Action Plan   22
Providing Congregational Care
and Support   22
    Evaluate the Congregation's
    Current Approach   22
    Set Priorities   23
    Build Congregational Care Capacity 23
    Evaluate Existing Care Models   24
    Create a Congregational Care
    Action Plan   26
Providing Support Through Worship   26
    Evaluate Current Offerings   26
    Ideas for Weekly Worship   27
    Incorporate Liturgical and
    Expressive Arts   27
    Ensure That Worship Is Accessible   27
    Create a Worship Action Plan   28

Providing Effective Communication   28
    Evaluate the Current
    Communications   28
    Integrate Your Communications   29
    Create a Communications
    Action Plan   29
Providing Supportive and
Accessible Space   30
    Evaluate Your Building
    and Grounds   30
    Visual and Artistic Support   31
    Create Accessible Space
    and Services   31
    Create an Action Plan for Space   32

The faith community
cannot be confined
within the house of worship.

It must stretch out to provide
a compassionate presence anywhere—
even in the "abyss of mystery"—
so that no one will die alone,
unattended, unwanted, unheard,
unseen or unloved.

FROM *COMPASSION SABBATH RESOURCE KIT*,
CENTER FOR PRACTICAL BIOETHICS, 2000

To provide feedback
on this toolkit, go to
www.iceol.duke.edu.

Unbroken circles of care begin with a vision that faith community members—children, teens, adults and older people—will be fully honored and supported through the seasons of illness, end of life and grief. Faith communities have a significant opportunity to offer essential support through fully prepared leaders and members—and through education, congregational care, worship, communications and accessible facilities. In addition, congregations have the opportunity to learn from people living with these challenges and to evolve by learning about the experiences they offer.

This chapter and those that follow will help you move from vision to reality. They include program ideas, resources, stories and quotes to help you create an unbroken circle of support around illness, end of life and grief, including ways to:

- teach leaders to understand the nature, impact and dynamics of these seasons of life

- educate members of all ages so they will be better equipped to support themselves and others

- offer practical, emotional, spiritual and social support for people living with these challenges to keep them connected with community

- provide specialized spiritual care and support—including pastoral visits and varied approaches to congregational support

- incorporate the spiritual experiences of living with illness, end of life and grief into worship

- provide thoughtful communication to ensure widespread education, and

- shape your building and grounds to offer full access to members and create spaces for support.

Because each faith community is unique, you will need to customize an approach to fit your congregation based on individual factors such as size, demographics, beliefs and culture.

Envisioning an Unbroken Circle

This chapter offers important steps for you to take as you evaluate your current ministries and plan and prepare new ones. The steps are organized around the areas of congregational life that relate most directly to creating an unbroken circle of support for people living with illness, end of life and grief.

Leadership

Few clergy have had formal education or ministry development training around illness, end of life and grief. In addition, few lay leaders have learned how to offer the education, congregational care and worship opportunities needed to support people living with these challenges.

This chapter includes strategies that clergy, faith community nurses and lay leaders can use to explore their

The world is round and the place which may seem like the end may also be only the beginning.

Ivy Baker Priest,
Political Activist

own experiences and to evaluate how effectively their congregations currently offer support. It provides strategies and tools congregations can use to create action plans for becoming unbroken circles of care. This chapter also offers helpful ideas and resources clergy and lay leaders can use to develop their knowledge and skills.

Education

While most congregations consider education to be an essential ministry that helps members develop their faith and understanding, few take a planned approach to education around illness, end of life and grief. Providing educational opportunities can help members better understand the many ways these seasons of life affect every person and his or her faith. Education helps members plan for living through these seasons, anticipating the needs that will come—a hallmark of an unbroken circle of care.

This chapter offers approaches and tips that clergy, faith community nurses, education committees, health ministry committees and teachers can use to integrate illness, end of life and grief into the congregation's educational ministry.

Congregational Care and Support

Congregational care and support is at the heart of creating an unbroken circle of care. However, many congregations currently rely on the crisis response model when reaching out to those in need. (See A Call to Action, pages 2 and 6 for more on this.) Clergy often become overextended and lay leaders and members often wonder how to offer the most effective support.

This chapter includes a congregational care self-assessment and models for building caring capacity for clergy and congregational care leaders and committees.

Worship

Although worship is often the central experience in faith community life, few congregations have thoughtfully planned how to fully integrate the seasons of illness, caregiving, end of life and grief into worship. While prayer is powerful, more can be done to offer support and to include members during these challenging times.

This chapter outlines ideas that clergy, lay leaders and worship committees can use for extending support through worship.

Communication

Congregations rely on effective communication to help support community life. However, few take advantage of communication strategies and tools already in place to extend community. And fewer still take creative approaches to designing communication strategies for people living with illness, end of life and grief.

This chapter addresses these missed opportunities and offers tangible suggestions that faith community nurses, health ministry committees and communications teams can use in reaching out.

Faith Community Space

While many faith communities have made strides in building and adapting facilities to be more accessible, many roadblocks still remain—especially for members facing illness and the end of life. In addition, faith communities have the opportunity to design new, creative spaces that offer ministry and support for people living with illness, end of life and grief.

This chapter highlights ideas for adapting and designing space for clergy, facility staff and building and grounds committees.

Supporting Others During Specific Seasons of Life

While this chapter offers general guidance for creating unbroken circles of care, each chapter that follows hones in a particular season of life—providing an overview of the season and then program ideas, practical tools and resources to help specifically with illness, end of life and grief.

Illness

Be mindful that you are pioneering in a world in which most people will live with illness for extended periods of time and many will be called upon to provide care for them. The information offered here will help your congregation recognize a day when each member will be affected by illness and be fully prepared to respond.

End of Life

Be creative as you weave issues related to understanding and preparing for death and dying into the fabric of congregational life. Through your efforts, you will help members grow in their own understanding and beliefs around end of life issues, equip them to plan specifics such as final medical care and funeral and memorial arrangements and be fully present with one another during this important time.

Grief

Be thoughtful as you prepare and plan outreach to grieving members of the faith community, remembering that the more congregations are able to normalize the grief experience and offer opportunities for mourners to express themselves, the more effectively they will be able to come to terms with their grief and faith.

Getting Started

Effective leadership is key to achieving the vision of a congregation becoming an unbroken circle of care for people living with illness, end of life and grief. As you prepare to lead your congregation, first explore your personal experiences with these issues, examine your congregation's current and changing demographics and assess your current capacity for ministry. This will lay the foundation for you to evaluate new ministry possibilities and to make an action plan.

Explore Your Own Experience

A key first step in preparing to lead is self-evaluation. The GUIDE FOR LEADER SELF-EXPLORATION, below, will help you probe and discover your personal experiences. The questions it contains may be explored individually, by recording thoughts and feelings in a journal, or in conversation with another leader or in a staff or leadership meeting setting. Your responses in each of the three areas will help you evaluate your own strengths and areas for growth as you prepare to lead others in creating unbroken circles of care and support.

GUIDE FOR LEADER SELF-EXPLORATION

Focus on one season—illness, end of life or grief—and explore your personal experience in relation to that season. Ask yourself:

ABOUT CHILDHOOD

What is my earliest or most profound experience with illness, end of life or grief as a child?

How did the adults around me respond?

What did I learn from this childhood experience?

How did it influence the ways I deal with this season as an adult?

ABOUT YOUR ADULT LIFE

In my adult life, what experience with illness, end of life or grief has been the most profound or challenging?

What was helpful for me during that time?

What was not helpful for me?

What was missing for me?

What have I learned about supporting others through that experience?

ABOUT YOUR LIFE NOW

Am I experiencing this season now?

How do I support myself through this season now?

How am I preparing myself for dealing with this season in the future?

How does my current growth and development affect how I support others?

When you finish, you may choose to begin your self-exploration again with another season until you explore all three. Be mindful that this inventory may bring up strong thoughts, emotions or memories, so find a way to express your reactions in healthy ways—through recording them in a journal, discussing them with friends or doing some activity such as exercising or gardening. By conducting your personal inventory, you will tap into your own understanding and experience as well as identifying your own areas for learning and healing.

Keep in mind it is normal to have more experience with one season than with another. For example, you many have significant personal experience with grief, but little direct experience with people who are near the end of life. Taking the time to explore the questions offered here will help you be clear about how you approach these different seasons in your own life and will also prepare you to lead your congregation in planning unbroken circles of care around them.

Evaluate Your Congregational Trends

A second step in developing leadership is to examine your current congregational demographics and trends. This is especially important given the reality that as the Baby Boomer generation is aging, people are living longer due to advances in medical treatment. As a result, the aging population in the United States will only continue to grow in coming decades. Faith community membership will also age along with the population.

Understanding your congregation's trends is important when creating unbroken circles of care now and when planning for the future. The DEMOGRAPHIC SCORECARD on the next page can be completed by an individual or a leadership group. While you may not know the exact number of people affected, make the closest approximation possible. While accurate estimates are important, the numbers need not be exact to reflect your current trends.

DEMOGRAPHIC SCORECARD
FOR CONGREGATIONS

Completing this scorecard will help give you a context for planning how to best support people currently experiencing illness, end of life and grief. And by comparing the current and expected demographic, you will see a more complete picture of your congregation's future.

How many congregation members are living with illness?

Total number: _____

Number of women: _____

Number of men: _____

Number living alone: _____

How many are facing the end of life?

Total number: _____

Number of women: _____

Number of men: _____

Number living alone: _____

How many are grieving due to the loss of a loved one?

Total number _____

Number of women: _____

Number of men: _____

Number living alone: _____

What is the age range of your congregation?
How many members do you have who are age:

0-18 _____

19-39 _____

40-59 _____

60-79 _____

80-89 _____

90+ _____

How does your demographic compare to 10 years ago?
To 20 years ago?

Based on your changing demographic, how do you expect your congregation will look 10 years from now?
How about 20 years from now?

**When the Mirror
Reflects Your Age**

For many, an honest demographic analysis will reveal a portrait of an aging congregation. Along with aging will inevitably come an increase in the level and frequency of serious illness, death and grief among faith community members.

Unfortunately, when some congregational leaders engage in such an analysis, their primary conclusion is that they must change the demographics. If, for example, there are more members who are aging and living with illness and fewer young people, the leadership may respond by saying: "We need to bring in more young families with children like we used to have."

While bringing in younger generations and raising children and teens in faith is vitally important, it is not the only answer for maturing congregations. Rather than focusing on maintaining a youthful image, the more pressing concern may be for congregations to offer meaningful ministry through education, care, worship and communication for people challenged by illness, end of life and grief.

GUIDE FOR CONGREGATIONAL SELF-EXPLORATION

Consider the following questions:

ABOUT CURRENT MINISTRIES

In what ways does our community of faith support people who are living with illness, end of life and grief through education, congregational care, worship, communications and in our buildings and grounds?

ABOUT CURRENT ROLES

What roles do our clergy, faith community nurses and lay leaders currently take on?

What roles do our members take on to support these people?

ABOUT CURRENT SYSTEMS

What systems does our faith community have to ensure that people in need receive consistent support over time?

Do these systems fit with the realities of the situations?

ABOUT THE LEADERSHIP TEAM

Who should be involved in learning and planning?

Are there key committees that can help with implementing plans for supporting people—for example: education, health ministries, congregational care, worship, children's ministries, building and grounds?

What talent do we have in our congregation or community already that may be tapped?

How can we best engage members who are living through these seasons of life to be part of the leadership development process?

ABOUT NEEDS FOR LEARNING AND GROWTH

What do our faith community leaders need to learn to effectively support members who are living with these challenges?

What strategies to learning will best fit our situation? (For ideas, see the discussion that follows.)

What organizations and agencies do we already know about that offer resources or might partner with our faith community to support members?

While you may decide to complete this assessment individually first, the most effective way to create change will be to bring leaders together to explore these questions. Your responses to these questions will become a basis for identifying areas of learning and growth and discovering unmet congregational needs.

Evaluate Your Congregation's Current Offerings

In addition to exploring your own experience, it is important to assess your congregation's current offerings in supporting members through illness, end of life and grief. As with the self-exploration questions on page 12, begin with one season and explore it with the GUIDE FOR CONGREGATIONAL SELF-EXPLORATION at left. When you finish, start again with another season if you choose until you consider all three.

Creating Action Plans

As you consider the key congregational areas of leadership development, education, congregational care, worship, communications and facilities, the following sections will offer general guidance for evaluating current ministries, learning about models for ministry, strategies and resources for creating circles of care, as well as important key steps in planning, implementing and reassessing ministries.

You may begin by focusing in one area for improvement or by working with different groups or committees to create change in several areas of congregational life. No matter where you choose to start, remember that you cannot be expected to do it all.

As you develop specific plans for offering new programs and ministries related to the seasons of illness, end of life and grief in key areas of congregational life, the following planning tools will help you organize. The ACTION PLAN TEMPLATE filled out as an illustration on the next page is a tool to help you focus efforts in a specific area. For example, your education committee may decide to offer a five-part educational series for adults on grief; you may then use this tool to develop your plan, building on the tools and resources included in this toolkit. Piloting individual ideas and programs in one of these areas may be your first step in meeting needs and building energy for change.

SAMPLE

ACTION PLAN TEMPLATE

Areas of Congregational Life (Check all that apply):

_____ Leadership Development   __X__ Education   _____ Congregational Care

_____ Worship, Music, Arts   _____ Communications   _____ Facilities

Season of Life (Check all that apply):

_____ Illness   __X__ End of Life   _____ Grief

What is the goal? *We will offer an adult education series to help members learn about end of life choices and plan ahead, emphasizing decision-making based on beliefs and values. We will include legal, financial, health care and funeral/memorial service planning.*

Why is this goal important? *Many members have questions about end of life planning for themselves, aging parents or others. We want to help members understand what our faith tradition believes about end of life choices and support them as they evaluate and prepare for end of life choices that honor their spiritual and religious beliefs.*

Who is responsible for ensuring that the goal is achieved?
Our adult education committee will be responsible for planning this series.

Who needs to be involved in the planning?
Members of the education committee will work with clergy and key content experts in our congregation and community to plan this series.

What is in place that will help us reach this goal?
We had a tradition of offering a 5 part educational series each year during Lent. This series will be an excellent fit for Lent next year.

What tools and resources from *The Unbroken Circle* **and other sources will we use?** *Pages 71-75 of the toolkit as content for a session on the advance care planning process, highlighting the role of spiritual beliefs and values in planning. We will also use information from Caring Connections, www.caringinfo.org, as a resource for legal, financial and health care decisions. The educational session "Planning a Funeral or Memorial Service" on page 78 as a guide for a session on that topic. The workbook "Getting It Together" on page 79 as a resource to help members organize legal, financial, health care and funeral/memorial service decisions.*

What additional information, content experts or partners are needed? *We will seek an elder-law attorney well-versed in end of life issues and current on our state's laws and documentation. We will seek a financial planner who specializes in end of life issues. We will seek a physician or nurse through our local hospice, end of life care coalition or hospital who can help use learn about the physical process of dying. We will consult with our local funeral/memorial society for planning the session on funerals and memorial services.*

What actions are needed to accomplish this goal? Include the timeframe for each.

Timeframe:	4-6 months in advance	3-4 months in advance	2-3 months in advance	During Lent
Action:	Order planning material samples	Invite guest speakers	Meet with all speakers	Offer series
	Determine series content and title	Develop publicity	Order materials to distribute	
			Publicize to congregation	

Are there key launch dates for this goal (for example: Educational Series, Special Worship, Support Team Launch, etc)? *Series will launch the second Wednesday in Lent.*

When will we check in on our progress? *We will check in during our regular Educational Committee meetings.*

What might keep us from accomplishing this goal? *Not planning far enough in advance.*

What can we do to help ensure success? *Check on our progress regularly at scheduled meetings.*

When will we evaluate what we have accomplished and plan next our steps?

In the month following the series, we will evaluate the impact using the Tool for Reassessing on page 16 and discuss our next goal in illness, end of life and grief as an education committee.

While some congregations will be ready to begin by piloting one action plan at a time, others will have the membership, staffing or volunteer infrastructure to start by planning for change in several areas of congregational life.

If you are creating action plans that affect different areas of congregational life during one year, use the CONGREGATIONAL ACTION PLAN ANNUAL OVERVIEW on the next page as a helpful tool. Consider establishing an overarching goal for the year, such as: "Our congregation will take a comprehensive approach to evaluating and improving the ways we support members living with illness."

To begin, you may form a leadership team or use an existing group, such as a church council or other coordinating body to decide on strategic areas for change. For example, the edu-

cation committee may take on making an action plan to offer educational sessions for adults and teens on how to support people living with illness. The congregational care committee may evaluate and implement new models for congregational care. The worship committee may plan a special service to support people living with illness. The staff or volunteers working on communications may integrate information around illness into the website and newsletter. The facilities committee may plan to make your space more welcoming to people living with illness.

The Congregational Action Plan Annual Overview, as demonstrated by the completed sample on the next page, will help you organize different plans, summarizing goals and key target dates. By attaching your specific action plans, you will have an organized way to track your efforts for the year.

Clergy, the leadership team or other coordinating body can use the overview to check in on progress quarterly and to plan a recognition and celebration of accomplishments and growth annually. These leaders can also use the overview to help chart the course for planning the next year, setting a new annual goal or expanding on the work accomplished the year before. Use the TOOL FOR REASSESSING below to evaluate your progress as a congregation and to identify new areas for planning and growth.

As you coordinate efforts in key areas of congregational life, growing your ministries in these key seasons of life, your congregation will move closer to the vision of becoming an unbroken circle of care for people living with illness, end of life and grief.

A TOOL FOR REASSESSING

In evaluating accomplishments and planning next steps, take time to celebrate the work you have done and to look ahead to starting your next action plan.

As you assess your work, ask yourself questions including:

Have we achieved our goal?

In what ways are clergy, lay leaders and congregation members better educated, prepared or supported around illness, end of life or grief?

What have been the benefits of our efforts related to this action plan?

What efforts are still needed to grow and develop our ministry goal?

What additional resources do we need to continue learning, serving and growing?

What is our next goal?

By reassessing your progress, your actions plans will build effectively on one another as you foster an evolving unbroken circle of care.

SAMPLE

CONGREGATIONAL ACTION PLAN ANNUAL OVERVIEW

Vision: Our congregation will become an unbroken circle of care
for people living with illness, end of life and grief.

Congregation: _The Unbroken Circle Congregation_   Year: _2010_

Overarching Goal for the Year: _One or more new ministries around illness, end of life and grief._

Key Area	Annual Goal — State the goal from each action plan.	Action Plan Completed — Check targeted areas. Attach plans.	Launch Dates — Educational Series, Special Worship, Support Team Launch, etc.			
			1st Quarter	2nd Quarter	3rd Quarter	4th Quarter
Leadership Development						
Serious Illness						
End of Life	A retreat for leaders to explore end of life issues				10/24	
Grief						
Education						
Serious Illness	Education on supporting people living with illness	yes			9/10	
End of Life	A Lenten series on end of life planning	yes (see sample)	3/1			
Grief						
Congregational Care						
Serious Illness	Pilot Support Team model	yes			9/15	
End of Life						
Grief						
Worship, Music, Arts						
Serious Illness	A service to support people living with illness	yes	3/4			
End of Life						
Grief	A Service of Remembrance	yes				12/14
Communications	Online resource center around illness, end of life and grief	yes		4/1		
Serious Illness	See above					
End of Life	See above					
Grief	See above					
Facilities						
Serious Illness	Evaluate our space and propose a plan to make it welcoming	yes	1/15			
End of Life						
Grief						

Providing Leadership Development

One of the greatest challenges faith communities face is how clergy and lay leaders can best provide consistent, comprehensive support for members who are living through the challenges of serious illness, end of life and grief.

Ill members may be scattered among hospitals or long-term care facilities across cities, counties or states—and some may live at home for months or years with limited energy and mobility.

End of life presents a particular challenge: Many clergy are self-

taught regarding end of life issues and have had to learn about caring for dying people from experience, through trial and error. In most congregations, lay leaders are in the same boat; few have received formal training related to death and dying. And helping grieving congregants not only takes time, but the ability to reach through isolation to those who do not have family, friends, professionals or a sensitized faith community around them to hear their stories and to respond with empathy.

All the individuals affected by these issues have complex needs, affecting not only themselves, but their family members and friends as well.

Assess Ideas and Resources

The leader and congregational self-exploration tools on pages 12 through 14 will help clergy and lay leaders identify important areas for learning and growth. To better equip both clergy and lay leaders in these areas, make a plan specifically for leadership development. Begin by assessing the types of leadership development activities that fit each leader's learning style. Some options are described here.

Self-Study

Clergy and lay leaders may use the toolkit and additional resources recommended in the specific chapters on illness, end of life and grief to learn more about selected topics for learning and growth. You may take a self-guided learning retreat or dedicate study over time. Your self-study may focus on areas you find most challenging—such as exploring theological concepts of illness and suffering, or what to say to someone who is dying or grieving following a suicide.

Study Groups

A group of clergy or lay leaders may come together to learn more about issues such as the effect of serious illness on children and their families, and burial rituals in their own or other traditions or particular types of grief. The additional resources listed throughout this toolkit will be helpful for planning this kind of study and in sparking discussion.

Planning Groups

As an alternative to a study group, convene a planning group to evaluate how your congregation can best support members facing serious illness, end of life or grief. This group may cut across existing committees—including representatives from adult and children's education, health ministries, congregational care, worship, music, building and grounds and so on. It

---

Help for Faith Community Leadership

It is increasingly clear that faith community leaders cannot be expected to take on the challenge of supporting members alone—and that congregations cannot expect staff to provide all the help they need. For congregations to become unbroken circles of care, clergy, faith community nurses and lay leaders must work with all members to develop a new understanding of what it means to live with illness, end of life and grief.

This toolkit can help you assess your own strengths and limitations related to these issues. It will encourage you to explore your own experiences, feelings and thoughts about them—and importantly, to consider how your congregation currently approaches leadership development in these areas. It will then offer direction and resources to help you think critically about how you can bring your congregation together to provide care and support. It will also help prepare you to teach and lead others to extend the circle of care to other members during these difficult seasons of life.

These needs become especially acute as the populations of faith communities age. According to the National Congregation Study, led by Duke University professor Mark Chaves, congregations are aging at a faster pace than society as a whole. In addition, congregational leadership is also aging. Between 1998 and 2006, the median age of clergy jumped from 48 to 53, a five-year increase, while the average age of the American public only increased one year in the same period.

Congregations will need to increase support for members who are ill or near the end of life—and to step up to meet the needs of those who are grieving. There will also need to be an increasing number of lay leaders and members trained in issues surrounding death and dying. Faith community leaders must be ready to help them develop their gifts and talents in providing support.

could also be an existing committee, such as health ministries, a deacon board or a leadership council. In forming a planning group, consider how best to include members who have been personally affected by illness, end of life and grief to make sure the plans you create meet the congregation's true needs.

Community Resources

Most communities have numerous resources available to help clergy and lay leaders learn more about illness, end of life and grief. While finding the most fitting may take some perseverance, the effort will be worthwhile. Not only will you access important information, you may also find individuals and organizations willing to provide expert speakers and content for the programs and communications you will offer. Some communities have end of life care coalitions that actively seek to involve faith community partners. (For a list of these, go to www.caringinfo.org.)

A number of additional community resources are described below.

Health care professionals. Clergy and lay leaders may consult with faith community nurses and other health care professionals to learn more about illness, end of life and grief. Faith community nurses, hospice staff and hospital personnel often welcome the opportunity to help others gain a deeper understanding of these issues at the intersection of health and faith. You may also attend local meetings of faith community nursing networks, access resources from local hospitals and organizations and attend conferences related to health ministries and faith community nurses.

Educational programs and support groups. Many community agencies offer programs and resources related to particular illnesses, end of life and grief. For example, most local chapters of the Alzheimer's Association conduct support groups, and many medical centers and hospices sponsor workshops on a range of relevant topics. By attending events hosted by community agencies, faith community leaders benefit from learning about the issues and illnesses that their members may be facing—and also from networking and establishing relationships with these organizations.

Leadership Conferences

More denominations are developing training conferences and events that relate to supporting people living with illness, end of life and grief. Check with regional and national contacts to learn about opportunities.

Some divinity schools and health organizations also offer national and regional conferences, including:

- Duke Institute on Care at the End of Life—www.iceol.duke.edu

- Project Compassion—www. project-compassion.org, and

- National Hospice and Palliative Care Organization—www.nhpco.org.

Create a Leadership Action Plan

After considering your options for leadership development and exploring the resources in the season specific chapters on illness, end of life and grief, make an action plan for leadership development using the ACTION PLAN TEMPLATE on page 15. You may decide to do two separate plans on each topic, one for clergy and another for lay leaders. Include these plans in your ACTION PLAN ANNUAL OVERVIEW (see page 17) and be sure to reassess at key intervals— at least once a year.

Providing Education for the Congregation

Few faith communities offer education for lay leaders and members on the physical, emotional, mental and spiritual impacts of serious illness, end of life and grief. As a result, affected members are often unprepared for the full impact these experiences can have on their participation in the congregation and the spiritual and other life changes connected to them. In addition, members who are not currently experiencing these challenges often do not understand the key issues involved. They remain unprepared to offer effective care and support for members experiencing these seasons of life.

Evaluate Current Programming

As you prepare to offer education in your congregation about illness, end of life and grief, first consider who needs to be involved in planning it. If you have separate committees for adult, teen and children's education, consider how best to involve them all—separately or together.

Whether you are clergy, a lay leader or part of a planning committee or taskforce, the GUIDE FOR ASSESSING EDUCATIONAL PROGRAMMING at right will help you with the important first step of assessing the current state of the educational offerings in your congregation.

Plan Future Programming

First determine topics you think are most important for your congregation to address immediately by using the GUIDE FOR ASSESSING EDUCATIONAL PROGRAMMING NEEDS at right.

If you are unsure about your congregation's educational needs, talk with your clergy, faith community nurse or congregational care leaders about spiritual issues that members bring up regularly with them. You may decide to facilitate a conversation about interests with existing adult education classes or to survey members about educational interests related to illness, end of life and grief.

Use Community Resources and Experts

As you focus on key areas for education, consider whether there are members in the congregation who have expertise in key areas, such as a hospice nurse or a hospital social worker. If you have a faith community nurse, talk with her or him about any interest in providing education around illness, end of life or grief.

If you do not have members with this expertise, seek out local organizations, agencies or experts in the community that would be willing to partner with you to offer education on these issues. (For more specific ideas on partnerships, see the following chapters on illness, end of life and grief.)

GUIDE FOR ASSESSING EDUCATIONAL PROGRAMMING

What education programs and materials do we offer for adults on serious illness, end of life and grief? How have these efforts been received?

What education do we offer that explores the spiritual aspects of these challenges?

What education do we offer for adults about how to extend care and support to others dealing with illness, end of life and grief?

What education do we provide for children about these topics?

What education do we make available for teenagers?

GUIDE FOR ASSESSING EDUCATIONAL PROGRAMMING NEEDS

ABOUT ILLNESS

How knowledgeable are our members about the course of diseases such as cancer, diabetes, Alzheimer's and dementia?

Are long-distance caregivers in our congregation informed about how to create support across the miles?

What spiritual concerns do our members face as they live with illness?

ABOUT END OF LIFE

Do our members understand the possible end of life services, such as hospice or hospital-based palliative care programs, that are available in our community?

What do our members know about advance care planning and the role faith can play in planning ahead?

What do our members know about our faith tradition's beliefs and traditions at the end of life?

ABOUT GRIEF

How informed are our members about the dynamics of grief?

How equipped are our members to support children and teens living with grief?

How prepared are our members to deal with traumatic grief following accident, violent death or suicide?

What spiritual concerns do our members face around grief?

Educational Opportunities for Children and Teenagers

To nurture a congregational culture that supports people of all ages around illness, end of life and grief, be sure to offer education for children and teens. Through periodic conversations and learning activities, adults can help children and teens learn about these seasons.

Sources that may spark learning include:

- stories from Scripture
- the nightly news
- a visit to a cemetery
- a dead plant, bug or animal
- the change of seasons
- a compost pile
- children's and teens' books
- movies, and
- visits with family members and friends who are ill.

By planning developmentally-appropriate educational programs for children or youth, you give them the opportunity to talk and ask questions about these issues in everyday settings, helping them understand death as a natural part of life.

You may also offer educational opportunities in combination with acts of service such as making cards for members who are seriously ill, planting a garden near your facility or visiting members who are homebound or in institutional settings.

Set a Calendar

While education on illness, end of life and grief can occur at any time of the year, consider what fits your congregation best based on the seasons, faith observances, health month observances or the liturgical year. For example, Christian congregations may plan an end of life program or series to coincide with Lent or Jewish congregations with Yom Kippur.

Consider how often your congregation will offer such education—for example, monthly or quarterly. You may offer a series or special study during the fall or spring. As you finalize your educational plan, put it on a calendar to make sure you are providing sufficient offerings and varying the topic areas.

Select a Format

As you explore options, consider that meaningful congregational education may occur in different formats.

Offering one-time educational sessions is one way to help lay leaders and members understand key issues that affect people who are dealing with illness, end of life and grief. Such sessions are an effective way to focus on one topic, test your capacity for offering this kind of education and spark interest and feedback for more extensive offerings.

But because issues surrounding serious illness, end of life and grief are so diverse, complex and often intense, a multi-part series covering these topics may be more appropriate than a one-time program. Such a series may give you the opportunity to explore topics more fully, develop deep relationships and build community with participants.

(See the chapters that follow for resources and references to several well-developed models for faith community educational programs to use or adapt.)

Presentation Is Everything: Tips on Effective Learning

Studies show that people learn more effectively through an interactive, participatory approach rather than by listening to lectures.

In fashioning your congregational education programs, consider how you can best:

- provide helpful information
- facilitate participation through experiential activities, and
- offer time for reflection, debriefing or discussion.

No matter how long or short your sessions, designate significant times for experiential activities.

One simple way to engage participants is to organize them into pairs or small groups and give them a few questions to discuss related to your topic. You can also have participants react to case examples, do roleplays, brainstorm possible ways to respond to a situation, draw "pain" or "grief," and so on. (For examples of interactive approaches, see the teaching sessions in the chapters that follow.)

Introduce Diverse Beliefs and Customs

Most people live in a diverse setting with neighbors, co-workers, friends and family members who practice different customs and faith traditions—and congregations can play an important role in educating members about them. Increasingly, faith communities also provide information and support for interfaith families seeking to learn about their loved ones' traditions and customs.

Consider offering one-time programs, a multi-part series or educational materials that address diversity among faith traditions and cultures surrounding illness, end of life and grief. For example, a Christian congregation may decide to work with a rabbi to offer a program on Jewish burial and mourning traditions. Consult the annotated resource list on the Duke Institute on Care at the End of Life website (www. iceol.duke.edu) as a starting place for locating resources.

You may also encourage neighboring faith communities to sponsor interfaith programs in which faith leaders can discuss these topics. These can also be good opportunities to partner with local hospices, which may be interested in helping to sponsor and organize such programs. One possibility is a panel of clergy representing Christian, Jewish, Islamic and Hindu traditions discussing how their faith traditions view death and the afterlife.

Promote Materials and Resources

Providing selected materials as part of educational sessions will give lay leaders and members easy access to information they can take with them. In addition to educational sessions, consider how your congregation can consistently offer instructive materials on serious illness, end of life and grief.

Some possibilities are discussed below.

Learning centers. Create a resource section in the library or media center by purchasing or asking members to donate books, DVDs and other resources contained in this toolkit or elsewhere. Provide resources for all ages—including children and teens.

Education boards or displays. Create a bulletin board or other display board to highlight aspects of illness, end of life or grief.

Factsheets and FAQs. Make targeted resources available, such as "Offering Spiritual and Emotional Support" and other consumer-orientated resources from Caring Connections (www.caringinfo.org) and other sources.

Create an Education Action Plan

Based on the ideas and resources provided in this chapter and in the education sections of the season-specific chapters that follow, make an action plan using the template on page 15. Include this plan as part of your Action Plan Annual Overview (see page 17) and be sure to reassess at least annually.

Providing Congregational Care and Support

Congregational care and support during seasons of illness, end of life and grief will help keep members connected with the faith community in significant, meaningful ways.

Effective congregational care will:

- support people throughout all stages—beyond an initial diagnosis or the days following a death or onset of grief

- respond to the diverse spiritual needs of people affected

- honor the many feelings and experiences that come with illness, end of life and grief

- recognize and respond to the practical, emotional and social needs people face

- offer a flexible plan of care that changes as members' needs change, and

- nurture the members' sense of belonging to the faith community.

For many faith communities, the essential challenge is to develop a comprehensive approach to congregational care and support that can be sustained. This section will help you assess your current plan for providing congregational care and support for members experiencing illness, end of life and grief. It will also help you plan for the inevitable transitions that members experience during illness and caregiving—anticipating needs and extending support to those in need.

Evaluate the Congregation's Current Approach

Using the GUIDE TO ASSESSING CONGREGATIONAL CARE AND SUPPORT on the next page, evaluate what your congregational currently does to support members experiencing illness, end of life and grief.

Consider bringing together a team of clergy and lay leaders to take the next steps of preparing and planning. You may choose to work with an existing group, such as a congregational care or health ministries committee. But do not limit yourself to your current circle. Involving some members of the congregation who have experienced illness, end of life and grief can help you conduct a more complete assessment of your current situation and make the most useful and fitting plan for the future.

GUIDE TO ASSESSING CONGREGATIONAL CARE AND SUPPORT

It is important to get a realistic reading of your congregational care for members experiencing serious illness, end of life and grief.

Ask the following questions:

ABOUT CURRENT CONGREGATIONAL CARE

What are our strengths in congregational care?

What types of support do we currently provide?

When and how do we offer this support?

ABOUT CRISIS V. NON-CRISIS RESPONSES

How do we offer care and support during critical times, such as hospitalization following surgery or the anniversary of a death?

How consistently do we offer care and support to members?

ABOUT ROLES FOR LEADERS AND MEMBERS

What expertise do our clergy have in supporting people during these challenging times? Our lay leaders? Our members?

Who organizes support for members?

Who provides the care and support?

ABOUT UNMET NEEDS

What are the key areas of improvement for our support?

To what extent does our current support fit with the need?

Do we extend community to our members rather than waiting for them to initiate contact with us?

What changes do we need to make to become an unbroken circle of care and support?

Set Priorities

You will likely determine that your congregation is strong in some areas and weaker in others. Agree on priorities in planning that will help you become more comprehensive in your approach to congregational care. Sample priorities to which your congregation could commit may include:

• responding to critical situations and transitions, such receiving a difficult diagnosis, dealing with an approaching death or breaking through the isolation of grief

• meeting a range of ongoing needs members face consistently

• combining the time, expertise and commitment of clergy, lay leaders and members

• facilitating communication of congregational caregivers so that members experience coordinated support, and

• sustaining congregational care efforts over time.

Because the challenges of illness, end of life and grief may affect many members in significant and varied ways, each plan will differ based on the congregation's size, demographics and situations presented.

Build Congregational Care Capacity

When building a congregational support system, one of the barriers congregations often face is the expectation that clergy will "do it all." Certainly there are times when a visit by the clergy person is expected, appropriate and significant. However, in some congregations, clergy visits have become the only tangible sign of support from the faith community some members receive. As a result, many clergy are stretched from crisis to crisis with little support.

As many exhausted clergy members have learned, doing more of the same thing seldom resolves a problematic situation; it often makes it worse. Instead, it is vital for clergy, lay leaders and members to work together to offer care and support—tapping into leaders' and members' diverse gifts and abilities.

It is important for clergy, lay leaders and members to develop a shared model for offering congregational care. Not only is a shared approach more manageable for clergy, it

Creating Capacity: Creative Approaches to Staffing

Congregations that are able to hire staff skilled in organizing, teaching and coaching lay leaders and members around illness, caregiving, end of life and grief benefit significantly from this investment—just as congregations that hire staff to work with youth benefit from the expertise that youth ministers may bring.

Savvy leaders will seek out staff with experience in nonprofit program development, community organizing, volunteer coordination and other related social service or community organizing fields as well as traditional ministry experience. People with backgrounds in parish nursing, social work, public health and other helping disciplines may be able to help with capacity-building as well.

If your congregation does not currently have the budget to hire such staff, be creative in engaging lay leaders and volunteers who have these skills. Lay leaders with these skills will help even small congregations build capacity.

As you plan, consider setting out a budget that incorporates staff and ministry resources to support people living with illness, end of life and grief.

engages lay leaders in meaningful ministry and communicates the full support of the congregation to members who are living with challenging conditions.

Equipping and supporting lay leaders and members to offer support is central to creating an unbroken circle of care.

This means investing staff or lay leader time in:

Program planning and coordination. Good program planning ensures that support is not hit or miss, but delivered consistently over time. And effective coordination ensures that everyone works together, not duplicating or overlapping efforts. It also ensures that roles are clearly defined and that program models are customized to fit the needs of those affected.

Orientation and ongoing learning. Clergy, lay leaders and members need orientation and ongoing education to fully participate in congregational care in helpful, appropriate ways. This includes follow-up education to help congregational care providers become proficient in providing support as situations change.

Communication. At the heart of effective congregational care is clear communication. Congregational care providers need to know and understand what support is needed and how they fit into the circle of care. Clergy, lay leaders and members also should be clear about how communication takes place, including how to incorporate emerging technology. Members need to understand the different roles clergy, lay leaders and members will take on, clarifying expectations for all involved.

Evaluate Existing Care Models

As noted above, because needs are so diverse, one approach to congregational care will often not be enough. Effective plans will often include more than one model. The major approaches are described below.

One-on-One Care by Clergy

The most common model for congregational care is for clergy to provide individual support to members. Often this includes visits and calls during critical times and also during routine periods of illness, end of life or grief—although this practice continues to decline.

Clergy should not underestimate the importance their visits and calls play in congregational care. Symbolically, clergy represent the congregation, conveying care and concern by their presence. Practically, they are often trained in congregational care issues, expected to speak in some way on behalf of the faith community on spiritual, ethical and religious matters. And functionally, clergy are invested with authority to offer rituals and sacraments offered by the faith—another tie to the community.

While it is important not to underestimate the power of effective clergy support, it is also important not to overestimate it.

It is essential for the planning group to discuss a number of questions, including:

- When are clergy visit and calls essential?

- When are clergy visits and calls preferred, but not essential?

- When are clergy providing visits and calls that lay leaders or members could provide instead?

- In what situations are members not experiencing support due to clergy limitations?

Honest answers to these questions will help open the door to developing lay leader and member models for support.

Clergy Support:
Too Much or Too Little?

A Methodist minister who serves an aging rural congregation 50 miles from two major medical centers observed he could spend all of his time on the road, going from one hospital visit to the next. He said he felt as if he were running in place, trying to see all his members multiple times in the hospital, not able to see them once they came home.

One solution could be to discuss expectations with the congregation and make a plan for him to involve volunteers.

For example, the minister could make an initial phone contact with the person and then visit once while the member is in the hospital. He could tell the hospitalized member that another member would check in by phone periodically or visit. The volunteer could alert the minister if the member needs an additional visit or if his or her condition changes. Members could also coordinate visits if the hospital stay is extended and when the person returns home, with periodic visits scheduled by the minister.

> *Even if your hold on God seems to slip at times, don't worry. God has a firm hold on you.*
>
> David Papp,
> *Stephen Ministries*
> *Program Director*

One-on-One Care by Lay Leaders and Members

Beyond short-term support such as meals or visits, some congregations formalize support by training volunteers and then matching them with members of the congregation who have needs. Members may provide companionship as friendly visitors, make check-in calls or help with meals or light housekeeping. Training and supporting volunteers helps them feel more confident and equipped to offer support. Some congregations design their own training. Others work in partnership with organizations such as Faith in Action programs. (For more information, go to www. fianationalnetwork.org.)

Some congregations train and support volunteers to provide one on one spiritual support including spiritual care visits, rituals and other support more often provided by clergy. Two Christian models of this approach to spiritual care are Called to Care, a lay caregiver program manual published by United Church of Christ Resources (800-537-3394) and Stephen Ministry (www.stephenministries.org). (Both are discussed in more detail in Support During Serious Illness, pages 48 and 49.)

The Team Approach

Adopting a team approach is another way to create unbroken circles of care for people experiencing illness, end of life and grief. A team approach allows congregations to significantly increase the level of support provided for members and their families, without requiring additional staff. While this approach is based on clear principles, it offers significant flexibility so that congregations can adapt models to meet their needs.

Several national organizations offer resources and support for congregations interested in adopting a team approach.

The Support Team Network. Support teams are groups of members organized to provide support—primarily for people living with illness, end of life or grief. Volunteers are asked to do what they enjoy doing, when they are able to do it, in a coordinated way and with a built-in support system. Using a team approach, lay leaders and congregation members pool their talents, creativity, time and leadership abilities to offer much more support than one volunteer can provide alone. Teams average six to 12 volunteer members and often have one or more volunteer leaders.

Their activities may include:

- practical support—such as help with transportation, respite, meals, errands, household tasks and yardwork

- emotional and social support—including visits, calls and check-ins

- spiritual support—such as spiritual visits, companionship, worship opportunities and rituals such as communion

- quality-of-life support—including social outings, gardening, help with hobbies, computer access, art projects, cookbook projects, pet care, and

- advocacy and resource support—tapping community resources, problem solving, accompanying individuals on doctor visits, organizing records and bills.

Teams can be created for individuals and families and can last for months or sometimes years as needs change. And they can also complement professional services, including palliative care or hospice services.

The Support Team Network offers resources for team development, including The Support Team Guidebook, leadership development conferences and consulting with individual congregations and communitywide coalitions. More information is available through Project Compassion at www. project-compassion.org or by calling 919-402-1844.

Create a Congregational Care Action Plan

After evaluating current approaches to congregational care, setting priorities and considering ways to build capacity and evaluating possible models for care, create an action plan or plans using the ACTION PLAN TEMPLATE (see page 15). Be sure to consider the program models and resources provided in this chapter as well as the ones included in the congregational care sections of the season-specific chapters. Incorporate this plan as part of your ACTION PLAN ANNUAL OVERVIEW (see page 17) and reassess it at least annually.

Providing Support Through Worship

While faith communities traditionally offer some forms of support for people living with illness, end of life and grief, few regularly integrate comprehensive congregational care into worship.

However, by taking the time and effort to do so, faith communities have tremendous opportunities to:

- encourage members to reflect on the spiritual and theological aspects of illness, end of life and grief beyond intercessory prayers

- engage members to consider these challenges through the arts and other creative expression in worship, and

- make worship approachable and accessible to those experiencing illness, end of life and grief.

Thoughtful worship planning anticipates the spiritual and theological matters all people face in living through illness, end of life and grief—and includes members as fully as possible as they live through these seasons.

Evaluate Current Offerings

The GUIDE TO ASSESSING CURRENT OFFERINGS offered here will help you with the important step of assessing how and whether your congregation currently incorporates the needs of those dealing with illness, end of life and grief into its worship offerings.

GUIDE TO ASSESSING CURRENT OFFERINGS

The worship team or committee may consider the following questions:

How does our worship support members experiencing illness, end of life and grief?

Do we regularly offer special worship opportunities for people living with these challenging conditions?

Do we consider all aspects of worship when offering support for these members?

Do we include liturgical and expressive arts as part of our planning?

How do we ensure that all people have access to opportunities regardless of their health?

Use these questions and others as a basis for creating a worship plan that incorporates support for people who are ill, dying or grieving—recognizing, honoring and normalizing the experiences that accompany these seasons of life.

Ideas for Weekly Worship

While faith tradition worship services and rituals vary, all may include opportunities for supporting members throughout the year. As you plan and adapt your weekly worship options, consider the following ideas.

- Scripture: Instead of bypassing a scripture or psalm in your cycle of readings that explores illness, end of life or grief, choose to include or focus on it.

- Readings and poems: Select readings from nonscriptural sources that tap into themes of illness, death and grief. Incorporate them into your worship. You can offer the readings and resources listed throughout this toolkit as a starting place.

- Children's sermons: Use children's books as a starting place for planning sermons for them that deal with illness, end of life or grief issues. (See pages 57, 85 and 96 for targeted resources.)

- Personal stories or testimonies: Create opportunities for members to share stories as part of worship. For example, Christian churches may consider a series of stories from members shared during Lent. Encourage people to bring out their struggles and questions as well as experiences of transformation and hope.

- Sermons: Draw on scriptures, books, movies, personal experiences and other sources to incorporate illness, end of life and grief into your sermons. Take on the topics in your sermons, empowering members to examine their own experiences of spirituality and these seasons of life.

Incorporate Liturgical and Expressive Arts

Many faith communities use the arts in worship and prayer as opportunities to extend care and support as well as to explore ideas and beliefs that words may not express.

Music. Music is a powerful way for people to feel supported during times of difficulty and strain. Include hymns and special music that address such issues during worship.

Dance. Some congregations have liturgical dancers who may offer a performance that reflects experiences of struggles with illness or grief.

Writing. Consider inviting people who are ill, mourning or grieving to share a poem or short piece of writing as part of a worship service.

Visual arts and crafts. Invite people who are ill, mourning or grieving to create pieces of artwork and share their thoughts about them during a worship service. Afterward, the artwork can be displayed in your facility. Some types of visual arts and crafts might be created during worship as a joint project by the congregants.

Theater. Drama can provide meaningful opportunities to address issues of illness, end of life and grief. A team or youth group may develop a drama or your congregation may perform existing dramas or readers theaters. (For more on this, see Vesta: Acting Out the End of Life, at right.)

Ensure That Worship Is Accessible

Worship can be difficult for people who are ill or grieving for many reasons.

Vesta: Acting Out the End of Life

Vesta is a one-act play that follows a matriarch named Vesta and her family members on a journey from wellness through aging, disability, dependence and loss. This intimate exploration of a family's journey through end of life incorporates humor and many of the challenging dynamics families face.

Written by Bryan Harnetiaux, the play can be performed as a stage production or a 90-minute dramatic reading. Audience talk-back sessions after the performance provide opportunities to discuss related issues such as advance care planning, caregiving and hospice. Congregations, hospices, divinity schools and coalitions have used Vesta to approach end of life issues in fresh, creative ways.

Vesta is distributed through the Duke Institute on Care at the End of Life at www. iceol.duke.edu/news/vesta. html. Complete production packets are available that include templates for advertising, director's notes and discussion guides.

Members may not feel well or may be concerned that a health-related issue could flair up during a service, that their bodies might do things that they cannot anticipate. Even when chronically ill people are physically feeling well enough to attend, they may be self-conscious about their appearances, limited mobility or the assistive devices that they need to use.

The desire for social isolation that can come with grief also makes it hard for many grieving people to be around others, particularly those who do not understand how to interact with them. Worship may also be difficult for those who have been away for some time because they were caring for another person or because they were accustomed to attending services with the person who died.

With these realities in mind, consider ways to keep those affected connected to the faith community.

Tapes or Podcasts

While many congregations dub tapes or burn CDs and distribute them to members who are unable to attend worship, it is important to keep "tape ministry" distribution lists current as people experience illness, treatment and other life-changing events. Clear communication between congregational care providers and tape ministry volunteers can help. In addition, more congregations now make recordings or podcasts of services available on their websites to ensure that worship is fully accessible.

Volunteers for Mobility and Respite

Congregations can organize volunteers to help members who need assistance in getting ready for and traveling to worship services. And

volunteers can also sit with people who are ill so that their caregivers can attend a worship service. Even if the congregation cannot make this commitment on a weekly basis, it might arrange to offer it monthly or bi-weekly. In providing this support, it is important to organize, train and support volunteers for their roles.

Worship Opportunities for Homebound Members

Many faith communities already consider ways to bring pieces of worship to those who cannot leave their homes. For example, some Christian pastors regularly bring communion to homebound members. And some Jewish volunteers participate in Shabbat observances with members in their homes. Be creative about how you can enable members to experience elements of worship when they are homebound. (See each season-specific chapter for ideas on specialized worship and for additional ideas on making your physical space more accessible.)

Create a Worship Action Plan

Once you have evaluated your current approaches to worship and explored new ideas for worship in this chapter and in the worship sections of the season-specific chapters, create an action plan using the ACTION PLAN TEMPLATE on page 15. Be sure to include that plan in your ACTION PLAN ANNUAL OVERVIEW (page 17) and to take the time to re-evaluate its effectiveness every year.

Providing Effective Communication

Through thoughtful use of communication, faith communities can integrate resources about serious illness, end of life and grief into everyday congregational life, helping to extend an unbroken circle of care to people living with these challenges.

Evaluate the Current Communications

Begin by assessing your current communication around illness, end of life and grief. Involve clergy, staff, your communications committee, health ministry committee or another related group.

Encourage those involved to ask:

- How do members of our congregation access information?

- What communication strategies do we currently use: Newsletters? Bulletins? Emails? Websites and other Web-based technology?

- How is our congregation evolving in the use of technology?

- What resources and support are we creating related to illness, end of life and grief that could be repurposed and communicated to members to build community and increase support?

- Are there times of the year when offering resources related to these issues would be a good alternative to providing an educational program or a special worship service?

Integrate Your Communications

As you explore communication options, consider the following possibilities.

Newsletters

For many congregations, newsletters are an obvious choice for communicating about issues, resources and messages associated with illness, end of life and grief. And there are many different ways to incorporate these topics.

Lead articles. Many faith community newsletters begin with an article written by the senior clergyperson. For example, an article that focuses on serious illness can communicate important messages about the issue and about how congregation members can help care for one another. Use the information in this toolkit as a starting point for writing an article. Such an article could stand alone—or be timed to coincide with a special worship service, an upcoming sermon, an education series or new congregational care efforts related to the issue.

Inserts. Whether accompanying a lead article or standing on its own, a newsletter insert can be a good opportunity to communicate information about illness, end of life and grief. For example, you may choose to include caregiving fact sheets such as those available on the website of the Family Caregiver Alliance (www.caregiver.org). You might choose to include a theological reflection about death. Or you may decide to include an insert such as "There is No Right or Wrong Way to Grieve After a Loss" available at www.nhpco.org/resources.

Tip sheets. Through your newsletter, you might provide information through articles and tip sheets written by a faith community nurse or lay leader or taken from this toolkit. These tip sheets can provide helpful suggestions related to caring for others who are ill, facing the end of life or grieving.

Stories and poems. Newsletters can provide an opportunity for faith community members to share their own wisdom, stories, poetry and artwork related to illness, end of life and grief.

Reviews of books and websites. Sometimes people can be overwhelmed by the many books, websites and other resources currently available. This toolkit will help you identify those that you can recommend. Congregants can share reviews through the newsletter, offering personal reflections about which ones were helpful and which ones were not. Reviews can also bring attention to resources that are available in your library or resource center.

List of resources. You may provide an annotated bibliography of books and movies related to illness and caregiving taken from this toolkit or provide a list of community agencies that offer support for people living with serious illness, end of life and grief.

Bulletin Inserts

Similar to newsletter inserts, bulletin inserts can be an effective way to bring attention to key messages about illness, end of life and grief. These inserts may tie in with a worship theme or health-related month, such as National Hospice Month in November. (For a sample bulletin insert series on advance directives, palliative care, hospice and bereavement, go to www.stjohns.org/palliativecare/faithleaders.)

Email

Some congregations send weekly or periodic email updates to members who have opted in to receive them. Consider integrating the strategies discussed above to enhance your email messages.

Websites and Other Web-Based Technologies

Few faith communities provide information about illness, end of life and grief on their websites; however, every congregation with a website should at least consider adding links to other resources likely to be helpful to its members.

For example, consider adding links to printable .pdfs of relevant tip sheets and other information that supplements what you provide in a newsletter. Also, offer links to relevant podcasts. And when your faith community hosts educational programs, consider recording them and making them accessible to people as a source that they may use as reference. Finally, don't overlook the obvious: links to other sites offering local and national information and resources. You will find many helpful websites referenced throughout this toolkit.

Create a Communications Action Plan

Once you have evaluated your current communications and explored new ideas, strategies and resources for communicating important information with your congregation, create an action plan using the ACTION PLAN TEMPLATE in this toolkit. (See page 15.) Include that plan as part of your CONGREGATIONAL ACTION PLAN ANNUAL OVERVIEW. (See page 17.)

As you integrate information and resources into your communications, reassess your progress and results regularly. As your communications evolve, be mindful about integrating information on illness, end of life and grief into your planning process, ensuring that a variety of information will be available to the congregation over time.

Providing Supportive and Accessible Space

Another easily-overlooked aspect of creating an unbroken circle of care includes modifying existing space or creating new space that fully includes people living with illness, end of life and grief.

Evaluate Your Building and Grounds

Bring together clergy, facility staff, buildings and grounds committees, arts committees or other related committees along with members who have experience with illness and disability to assess your current space. Use the GUIDE FOR EVALUATING BUILDING AN GROUNDS for guidance.

One way to increase support for people living with illness, end of life and grief is to provide in-kind space for hospices and other local organizations to offer public workshops or support groups. For example, the Alzheimer's Association might host a community workshop for caregivers on your site or a local hospice or hospital might need a community location for a grief group.

By making your building available to local organizations, you make the service convenient for your members and available to your community. You also build positive relationships with organizations that can assist with your efforts in extending circles of care.

Using Existing Space Creatively

While some faith communities use every square inch of space for classes and activities, others have extra offices, large closets or rooms that are available.

There are a number of creative ways these spaces can be used.

Resource spaces:
- an annex office of a local community agency, or
- a library and distribution center for educational materials related to illness, end of life and grief.

Respite spaces:
- a room where people who cannot attend worship can have companionship and basic care while their caregivers go to a worship service.

Storage spaces:
- a craft materials storage room for congregations that create prayer shawls or quilts
- room for donated medical equipment such as wheelchairs, walkers and bedside toilets that can be loaned or given to members, and
- an extra freezer to store donated food that can be taken to those who are living with challenging conditions.

GUIDE FOR EVALUATING BUILDING AND GROUNDS

Ask the following questions:

Do we offer available space to community groups and organizations that provide programs and services related to illness, end of life and grief?

Do we have unused rooms or storage areas to house our own ministries for people who are living with illness, end of life or grief?

Do we display artwork or photographs that reflect the themes of illness, caregiving, end of life or grief?

Do we have accessible parking spaces or drop-off areas for people who cannot walk long distances?

Are people with physical limitations able to access our facility safely and easily? Are there rooms or floors that are inaccessible to people in wheelchairs or to those who cannot climb stairs?

How many places are reserved for wheelchairs in our sanctuary? When people use those places, can they see and hear the worship services? Do they feel fully included in the congregation?

Are people with physical limitations involved in worship leadership? Are our altars, pulpits or other worship leadership areas accessible to people in wheelchairs or those who cannot climb stairs?

Do we offer hearing devices and large print bulletins and hymnals?

Provide an entry space to allow visitors to transition from a busy institutional environment to a calmer, warmer and more welcoming one.

Whole Building Design Guide: www.wbdg.org.

Visual and Artistic Support

Many congregations use artwork and visual displays to convey important messages and offer support. As you consider how to fully support your members, you may decide to incorporate:

- artwork made by people who are living with illness, end of life and grief

- prayer shawls and prayer quilts with information about the ministry and how to request one for a loved one (see pages 53 and 54 for more specifics on this)

- photographs and visual arts that include people at all stages in life

- bulletin boards with photos of and information about members providing caregiving support, such as support teams, and

- a temporary labyrinth where people can walk a symbolic journey and be engaged in walking meditations or centering times of prayer. Temporary cloth labyrinths can be borrowed, rented or constructed from materials such as lyme, cans, rope or surveyor's flags. Labyrinths can be made accessible for people using wheelchairs. To learn more about labyrinths or to locate one in your area, go to http://labyrinthsociety.org/home.

Create Accessible Space and Services

There are a number of steps you can take—from physically overhauling or reconstructing a space to adding simple touches—that can help make worship more accessible to all.

Physical Changes

Consider whether your physical space is physically accessible for people in wheelchairs and for those who have difficulty climbing stairs or walking long distances.

If your facility is not entirely accessible, you may need to be creative. If your main entrance is not accessible or adaptable, consider whether alternative routes might be adaptable. If you do make adaptations, be sure that they are clearly marked. If there is a long distance between a vehicle drop-off point and a door, you may wish to schedule volunteers to assist with wheelchairs or umbrellas on rainy days. If you have or install ramps, railings or elevators, mark directions clearly to help people find them.

As you consider how accessible your worship space is, be sure that a person in a wheelchair can move successfully from your entrance into your sanctuary. Testing this yourself can be a valuable exercise. You may consider removing chairs or pews to make room for wheelchairs. To make your sanctuary more accessible for people living with illness or caregiving, consider reserving seating spaces near entrances so people can come and go more easily.

Assess restrooms to ensure that they are accessible and safe. If they require retrofitting, work with an architect or builder familiar with accessibility adaption.

If your congregation is planning a new building, look beyond meeting the standards required by the Americans With Disabilities Act (ADA) and local laws to consider whether the design of the new building is inviting for people who have physical accessibility concerns. Consider whether your members and visitors will be able to access your entire facility. Build into the design full access to altars, pulpits, choirs and other worship leadership areas so that people living with illness and disability have easy access to all of them.

Other Changes

You can also often make simple, affordable changes to encourage an atmosphere and space that welcomes people.

For people with diminished hearing, assistive hearing devices, quality sound systems and sign language interpreters can help them participate fully.

For people with sight impairment, small modifications can make a big difference—including well-lit hallways, symbols and signs that clearly identify restrooms, elevators and doors and clear signage indicating important rooms such as your worship space or your community hall. Offering large-print bulletins and hymnals also ensures that you include people with visual difficulties. And for people who are blind, signs and hymnals in Braille can be helpful.

Access Resources to Help Transform Your Space

Many of the resources available for helping congregations become accessible for people with disabilities will help you in refashioning your space.

For example, the Family Village is a website for children and adults with disabilities, their families and their friends. It brings together thousands of online resources in an organized, easy-to-use directory. The centerpiece of Family Village is the library, where visitors can find information on more than 300 diagnoses. Visitors can also learn about assistive technology, legal rights and legislation, special education and leisure activities.

The Family Village Worship Center offers an extensive list of organizations sponsored by various faith traditions, ministries and denominations. For more information, go to www.familyvillage.wisc.edu/Worship.htm.

Create an Action Plan for Space

Once you have evaluated your buildings and grounds and explored new ways to make it more accessible and inviting, create an action plan using the ACTION PLAN TEMPLATE in this toolkit. (See page 15.) While some goals such as creating a temporary labyrinth may be accomplished in one year or less, goals that involve retrofitting facilities or building new ones may require multi-year planning as well as coordination with other committees. Be sure to include your action plans for space as part of your ACTION PLAN ANNUAL OVERVIEW (see page 17) and to reassess at key intervals, at least annually.

TOOLS FOR ACTION

The chapters that follow will help you build on the overarching strategies explored in this chapter, providing information, tools and resources specific to the seasons of illness, end of life and grief. Each chapter will help you customize your congregational action plan by offering:

- an overview of the specific season—illness, end of life and grief

- a primer about the topic with resource lists to help you deepen your knowledge and understanding, and

- an exploration of how to address each season through education, congregational care and worship.

Each chapter's sections on education, congregational care and worship includes:

- practical information—including sample education sessions, program ideas, tip sheets, exercises, handouts and other tools

- descriptions of proven models for ministry with instructions for creating them, and

- select lists of resources and organizations that also offer many helpful tools imbedded in them to help you improve education, congregational care and worship.

Taken together, each chapter provides a comprehensive array of tools for congregations of all sizes to create unbroken circles of care and support.

How This Toolkit Can Help 34

Changing Views of Illness 34

Illness as a Season of Life 35

Understanding Illness 35

The Impacts of Illness 36

Physical Impact 36

Emotional Impact 37

Spiritual Impact 37

Illness and Suffering 38

The Opportunities of Illness 38

Power to Grow 38

Power to Give 39

Power to Receive 39

Power to Advocate 39

Power to Lead 40

Living With Caregiving 41

Challenges of Caregiving 41

The Opportunities of Caregiving 42

Creating Unbroken Circles Around Illness 43

Illness Education 43

Educational Sessions 43

An Illness Series 47

Congregational Care 48

Visiting the Sick 48

Called to Care 48

Faith in Action 49

Stephen Ministries 49

A Team Approach 49

Support Groups 51

Adult Day Programs 52

Creative Support Ministries 52

Caring for Children and Teens 55

How Faith Communities Can Help 55

When the Patient Is a Child 55

Meeting the Needs of Ill People Through Worship 57

Special Worship Services 57

Worship for Those With Specific Illnesses 58

Special Seasons and Holidays 59

Weekly Worship 59

While my struggle with illness never defines me, it shapes my values, molds my perspectives and expands my capacity for gratitude.

It is true that I am not illness, but I will always be its student.

TIFFANY CHRISTENSEN, AUTHOR OF *SICK GIRL SPEAKS!*

To provide feedback on this toolkit, go to **www.iceol.duke.edu.**

A 93-year-old retired professor was talking with his daughter about his chronic health issues. "I thought I would live my life and then die," he said. "I wasn't expecting the in-between part." Few healthy individuals anticipate they will live with lasting challenges to their health. Fewer still expect they will be diagnosed with a life-threatening illness. Most people simply do not expect the "in-between part" that life so often delivers.

In time of illness, the soul collects itself anew.

Latin proverb

But in reality, the vast majority of Americans live with serious illness for a year or more before dying. Serious illness brings with it months or even years of physical, emotional, spiritual and social changes that significantly affect the quality of life for people living with illness—and those who care for them. Because the effects of serious illness are often long-term, is has become a full-fledged season of life.

Although chronic and life-threatening illness are clearly part of everyday life for an increasing number of their members, many faith communities remain unprepared for providing and sustaining support for their members during the "in-between" part of their lives. Still fewer are prepared to offer support for extended families, friends and others in their community beyond their membership.

How This Toolkit Can Help

This chapter will help you explore ideas and resources to support people living with illness. Specifically, it gives you structure and guidance to:

- develop your leadership so that you can teach others about issues related to illness

- educate members to equip themselves and others around illness

- explore and adopt models for providing congregational care, and

- integrate support for people living with illness into worship.

The information here will complement the strategies and ideas for leadership, education, congregational care, worship, communications and faith community space found in the earlier chapter, Creating Unbroken Circles of Care.

As you tailor ministries specifically for people and their families who are living with serious illness, your congregation will make a significant difference in the lives of all members— and make real strides toward becoming an unbroken circle of care.

Changing Views of Illness

To anticipate the needs of those affected and offer them effective care and support, clergy, lay leaders and members must first understand the dynamics of serious illness.

A few generations ago, Americans experienced serious illness much the same way their distant ancestors did. In the early 1900s, the average life expectancy was 50 years. Before antibiotics and other advanced medical treatments were developed, people usually died quickly of disease, infection or injuries from serious accidents.

But since the middle of the twentieth century, science and technology have transformed the American experience of illness and death. The medical system usually fights illness and disease aggressively with a wide range of treatments and medications. When options seem limited, many patients do not think twice before seeking out the latest therapies, experimental treatments, any medical form of hope available. Curing illness—and sometimes just extending life—have become primary goals. The life expectancy in the United States now exceeds 78 years, a number that rises in most locales every year. In sharp contract with our ancestors, Americans now expect that medical care will offer cures and treatments, no matter the illness, to enable longer lives.

Illness as a Season of Life

Ironically, by extending our lifespans, advanced medical treatments now almost guarantee that most Americans will live long enough to develop at least one chronic or life-threatening illness. A small percentage of the population is likely to die due to a sudden heart attack, accident, violent death or suicide. But most people—more than 90%— will likely experience a protracted, life-threatening illness before dying.

However, fueled in large part by rapid advancements of medical treatments and the new expectation that illness can be "managed," many healthy individuals maintain a false sense that they can avoid illness by doing the right combination of things. And television, movies, news, advertising and other media reinforce this impression.

The truth is that illness can come to anyone at any time and at any age. It often arrives through a sudden pain, a strange lump, a routine test, a sense that something is not right. The sudden diagnosis of a serious illness brings with it shock, surprise and an unexpected confrontation with mortality. Indeed, the diagnosis of a life-threatening illness is much more than a medical event: It is often nothing short of a life passage and the beginning of a new journey.

For many people, a new diagnosis feels overwhelming. Navigating the modern medical maze has become increasingly challenging as patients and their families face a wide range of treatment options. And increasingly, cost is another major factor, with significant variations in insurance coverage and access to care. Whether a person is dealing with a difficult diagnosis, going through treatment, losing function over time or facing life-threatening illness, there is no one clear path to follow. Unlike our ancestors a few generations ago, our relationship with illness is significantly more extended and complex.

Understanding Illness

Since nine out of ten Americans will experience chronic or life-threatening illness for months, years or even decades, it is important to strive to understand what it means to live with it. By learning more about the most frequently occurring illnesses, clergy and lay leaders will be better prepared to anticipate the challenges members face and provide informed education, congregational care and worship.

You can learn more information about chronic and threatening illnesses affecting members of the congregation from reliable sources such as the Center for Disease Control and Prevention (www.cdc.gov) and the National Institute of Health (www.nih.gov).

You can also learn more about illnesses, along with their causes, treatments and side effects, from illness-specific organizations. The most common illnesses, along with organizations offering specific information on them, include:

- Alzheimer's disease and dementia—Alzheimer's Association at www.alz.org

- Amyotrophic Lateral Sclerosis (ALS)—ALS Association at www.alsa.org

- Cancer—American Cancer Society at www.cancer.org

- Diabetes—American Diabetes Association at www.diabetes.org

- Heart disease—American Heart Association at www.americanheart.org

- HIV and AIDS—AIDS Info from the U.S Department of Health and Human Services at www.aidsinfo.nih.gov and The Body: The Complete HIV/AIDS Resource at www.thebody.com

- Kidney disease—National Kidney Foundation at www.kidney.org

- Parkinson's disease—National Parkinson Foundation at www.parkinson.org

- Respiratory disease—American Lung Association at www.lungusa.org and the National Heart, Lung and Blood Institute at www.nhlbi.nih.gov and

- Stroke—National Stroke Association at www.stroke.org and American Stroke Association at www.strokeassociation.org

Pain Care Bill of Rights

According to the American Pain Foundation, people with pain have to rights to:

- have the report of pain taken seriously and to be treated with dignity and respect by doctors, nurses, pharmacists and other health care professionals

- have their pain thoroughly assessed and promptly treated.

- be informed by their doctors about what may be causing the pain, possible treatments, and the benefits, risks and costs of each

- participate actively in decisions about how to manage the pain

- have the pain reassessed regularly and the treatment adjusted if the pain has not been eased

- be referred to a pain specialist if the pain persists, and

- get clear and prompt answers to their questions, have time to make decisions and refuse a particular type of treatment if they choose.

SOURCE: THE AMERICAN PAIN FOUNDATION (WWW.PAINFOUNDATION.ORG).

The Impacts of Illness

Illness is a complex phenomenon with many dimensions: physical, emotional and spiritual. While each person experiences disease and treatment in a unique way, the key factors, experiences and reactions discussed below are quite universal.

Physical Impact

The physical changes that come with illness cannot be overstated. Depending on the disease or condition, illness may bring challenging symptoms such as fever, chills, congestion, coughing, swelling, constipation, diarrhea and fatigue. These and other symptoms can have major impacts on daily life. Illness or treatment may also affect basic activities such as eating and sleeping. People may become unable to dress, bathe or feed themselves.

Many people living with illness have decreased energy, mobility and ability to work and care for themselves. This has a direct effect on how they perceive themselves, their roles and their contributions to the world around them.

In addition, physical symptoms affect family members and others who provide those who are ill with care and support. Often caregivers rearrange their work and home lives to offer help.

As a vital first step to offering care and support, it is essential for congregation members to understand the wide-reaching impacts of physical symptoms and side effects on people living with illness and their caregivers.

One significant and often misunderstood symptom that factors into many illnesses is pain. It is part of the body's defense mechanism, its way of communicating that something is wrong. A major

symptom in many medical conditions, pain can significantly interfere with a person's functioning and quality of life.

At any time, more than 25 million Americans suffer acute pain caused by infection, injury, surgery or other medical condition. And more than 50 million people suffer with chronic pain—a persistent pain that results from long term-illness.

Diagnosing pain is based on duration, intensity, type of pain, source, location in body and other factors. However, pain is a highly subjective experience, differing from person to person. One definition used widely in health care circles is: "Pain is whatever the person experiencing it says it is." Tools such as the commonly used "pain scale" ask people to rate their pain on a scale of 0 to 10, helping health care providers assess, treat and monitor a condition.

Along with the sensation of pain itself, unmanaged pain can bring along with it a number of symptoms such as impaired sleep or reduced appetite. It can take a toll on a person's mood, outlook on life, relationships and self-image. Unmanaged pain can be accompanied by anxiety, frustration, depression, difficult memories of previous pain experiences or the anticipation of pain yet to come. Pain can also interfere with a person's thought processes, decisionmaking and ability to address spiritual issues and questions related to illness. In some cases, it can even bring thoughts of suicide.

There are many ways to control pain, including a wide range of medications, radiation, and nerve blocks. Alternative therapies such as acupuncture, massage, aroma, music and other forms of therapy are also increasingly being used.

Emotional Impact

In addition to recognizing the physical signs and symptoms of illness, it is important for clergy, faith community nurses and lay leaders to be aware of the wide range of emotions that illness can provoke.

A few of the most common are described here.

- Disbelief. People may not believe the diagnosis or the progression of an illness or that the changes or symptoms occurring are connected with the illness.

- Fear. Some people may be fearful about what will happen as an illness progresses, and about what the future holds for them and for those close to them. Fear can arise again and again as an illness progresses.

- Anger. People who are ill may be angry for many reasons— including past treatment choices, a change in diagnosis, the progression of illness and the lack of understanding or support from the health care system, family members or faith community.

- Anxiety. People experiencing illness may also be anxious about many things, including facing new tests, making treatment decisions or lack of resources for care.

- Grief. People may experience a wide range of grief reactions— including deep sadness and longing—as they face the losses that come with illness. (To learn more about grief, see the chapter titled Support Through Grief.)

- Depression. Depression is one of the most common symptoms of chronic or long-term illness. While the nature and treatment of clinical depression is better understood today than in previous generations, its impact is still underestimated.

Spiritual Impact

Spiritual pain is as real and power-ful as physical and emotional pain. While spiritual pain may raise dif-ficult questions and doubts for peo-ple, it may also serve as a catalyst for spiritual healing and growth.

Although not everyone deals with the same spiritual issues, there are some that commonly arise as people struggle with an illness or help someone else through one:

Meaning and purpose. Many people who are seriously ill question what their lives mean. They may wonder if their lives have made a difference and question if they are still able to make contributions. Some people ask "Why me?" or "Why now?" or "Why this illness?" The search for meaning and purpose may bring up a wide range of emotions—from anger and loss to relief and peace.

Guilt and forgiveness. As people face illness, they may reflect on difficult situations and experiences from the past. They may experience guilt or blame others for things that have happened or ultimately seek forgiveness from others or from God.

A Closer Look at Depression

Up to one-third of those who have a serious medical condition experience symptoms of depression.

Common symptoms of depression include:

- loss of interest or pleasure in daily activities

- significant weight loss or gain

- sleep disturbances—sleeping too much or too little

- problems with concentration

- apathy—a lack of feeling or emotion

- feelings of worthlessness or guilt

- fatigue or loss of energy, and

- repeated thoughts of death or suicide.

Family members and medical professionals often overlook the symptoms of depression, assuming that it is normal for someone struggling with a serious illness to feel down. And symptoms of depression such as fatigue, poor appetite, impaired concentration and insomnia are also common features of chronic medical conditions, adding to the difficulty of deciding whether they are due to depression or to the underlying illness.

It is extremely important to treat both the depression and the chronic medical illness at the same time. Sometimes symptoms are improved by changes in the treatment of the illness or changes in medications. Sometimes depression medication or talk therapy is needed. Individuals and family members should be encouraged to work with professionals to identify depression and seek the most effective approaches to alleviating it.

Loss of faith. The losses that can come with illness cause some people to question their beliefs or faith. They may become angry with God, themselves or with others who think they should maintain certain beliefs.

Lack of support from religious tradition or faith community. As they live with illness, many people become disconnected from their faith tradition or community. They may lack the energy to keep the connection going. They may not know how to ask for support and some faith communities do not know how best to provide it.

A Closer Look at Palliative Care

While traditional medical care often focuses on cure, palliative care emphasizes caring for the physical, emotional and spiritual well-being of the patient and their family in the face of chronic and serious illness. Palliative care emphasizes the assessment and treatment of symptoms such as pain and suffering. It also includes coordination of care, crisis prevention and attention to grief.

While palliative care is often associated with end of life care, ideally it will be integrated into all aspects of care, even at the time of diagnosis.

To learn more about palliative care, go to www.getpalliativecare.org.

Illness and Suffering

Along with pain, illness often brings suffering. For theologians and philosophers, suffering raises the question of theodicy—the attempt to reconcile the existence of evil and suffering with the existence of God. Epicurus, the ancient Greek philosopher, framed the question as a paradox: "Is God willing to prevent evil but not able? Then God is impotent. Is God able but not willing? Then God is malevolent. Is God both able and willing? Why, then, evil?"

Theological and philosophical discussions on the nature of suffering and evil abound. Through the centuries, theologians have suggested theories such as:

- Evil and suffering result from disobeying God or from sin

- Suffering is an illusion

- Suffering brings redemption

- Suffering exists so that God can create good through it

- Suffering is a test of faith, and

- God suffers with us.

People living with illness may explore some of these and other thoughts about suffering. When a person is ill, these thoughts are not abstract concepts or intellectual exercises, but rather intense personal experiences. Part of supporting people though suffering includes listening to their experiences and offering support as they wrestle with questions of suffering and belief.

While there are many ways to understand suffering, one helpful description comes from physician Eric Cassell. He says suffering occurs when a person feels his or her sense of self is threatened. According to Cassell, suffering continues until

the threat passes or the person re-establishes a new sense of self in the face of suffering.

The physical, emotional and spiritual impacts of illness can create this feeling of threat to the sense of self and bring deep suffering. While each religious tradition interprets suffering differently, part of helping people experience relief from suffering involves listening to the source of suffering and helping people find a renewed sense of meaning, purpose or healing in relation to God, themselves or others in the midst of the threat.

The Opportunities of Illness

While it is essential to understand the issues, challenges and suffering that illness can bring, it is equally important to explore the opportunities for growth and change it offers.

Power to Grow

Experiencing illness can help force people to clarify what matters most to them in life. It can challenge people to tap into undiscovered or underdeveloped talents and abilities. Illness can encourage people to grow in faith and develop their spiritual lives and disciplines. And it can prompt them to focus on relationships that need healing or on goals they want to achieve.

For example, following a diagnosis and treatment, postal carrier Jeffrey Moore said: "Illness gave me a whole new perspective on life, a new sense of urgency to create. Now I'm making independent films, writing books." And as one faith community nurse said of the experience with illness: "In retrospect, cancer became one of the greatest gifts I've ever experienced."

Power to Give

The desire to give is part of the human condition. While some individuals living with illness may not be able to give in the same ways they have in the past, their illnesses may inspire them to find new ways to help others. For example, a woman who loved to cook reached a time in her illness when she was no longer able to make her signature dishes. She made copies of selected recipes and gave them to family members and friends as a way for them to remember her and her cooking.

Power to Receive

American culture, including faith community culture, often fosters an independent mindset that makes it difficult for people to ask for assistance. One gift of illness can be that people become open to asking others for the help they need.

Cicily Saunders, the founder of the modern hospice movement, described adjustments she and her husband made in their own lives some years before her husband's death when he needed help with simple tasks of daily living, such as getting dressed and going to the bathroom. Even through others attended to his most personal needs, he found the power to receive support without diminishing himself. According to Saunders: "He may have lost his modesty, but he never lost his dignity."

Power to Advocate

Whether people are moved to speak up to get the best health care possible or to have their wishes for care honored, illness can help them develop a new capacity to advocate for themselves. Increasingly, health care providers expect patients and families to assert themselves and help direct critical decisions in their care.

Three Keys to Patient Advocacy

At the age of six months, Tiffany Christensen was diagnosed with cystic fibrosis, a genetic illness that primarily affected her lungs. Since then, she has spent a majority of her life in in-patient hospital care and has received two double-lung transplants. Now a patient advocate, speaker, author of a book, *Sick Girl Speaks: Lessons and Ponderings Along the Road to Acceptance* and blogger at www.sickgirlspeaks.com, Christensen also works with Project Compassion in Chapel Hill, North Carolina, developing patient advocacy services and resources.

From the valuable vantage point of a patient, she offers three keys to becoming an effective advocate.

1. Knowledge

As a patient or a caregiver, the first step to getting the most from your health care is to know as much as possible about your illness, as well as your current and possible treatment options.

Access the Internet. The Internet offers medically technical sites for ambitious readers as well as general information sites written in simple terms designed by patients for patients and online support groups. Not everything you will read there will be completely accurate, but it is a good place to start.

Ask questions. Create an informational dialogue with the professionals caring for you. Encourage them to tell you about what they are doing as they do it.

Talk with other patients. A social worker, nurse or doctor will usually be glad to connect you with other patients who have traveled similar paths to the one that you are on now. Their experiences may be valuable in helping you face obstacles they have faced before you.

Keep records. If you keep a record of which medicines and treatments were helpful and which were detrimental, you will be able to guide your health care providers in giving you the best care.

2. Awareness

When we are sick, either as an outpatient or in the hospital, all we want to do is relax and let people take care of us. Don't relax too much! Staying aware of what is being prescribed and administered to you orally or intravenously can save your life.

3. Boundaries

Setting boundaries is difficult for many people, but it is a skill you will have to work to improve. If something is being done that goes against your understanding of your care plan, don't be afraid to insist on speaking with your doctor before anything resumes. Become a humble, polite and selective squeaky wheel.

Power to Lead

Some people describe illness as a teacher that has helped them learn about their own humanity, faith and beliefs, perspective on suffering, sense of quality of life.

For example, physician Michael McLeod, now retired, was diagnosed with an aggressive form of cancer in his late 50s, requiring surgery and treatment. "I had been trained as a rational scientist and I had developed this illusion of control, this belief that money and titles and material things really mattered," he says. "When I opened myself up to facing my own illness, my own possible death, I began to realize the fears that lay underneath the surface. Suddenly I began to be free of all the constraints that held me back from living fully."

The doctor-turned-patient reordered his priorities, spending more time with family and friends. He developed new hobbies and focused on his own spiritual growth. He developed a gratitude for the blessings in his life and an appreciation for every moment. In his retirement, he began teaching medical students what patients experience on the other side of the fence. As he now says: "My whole perspective on life began to change because of my illness. I now see life through a new set of lenses."

AARP: www.aarp.org

Nonprofit membership organization providing information, advocacy and resources for people age 50 and older. Topics covered include preventative health, long-term care options and family caretaking.

Being Well When We're Ill: Wholeness and Hope in Spite of Infirmity, **by Marva J. Dawn; Augsburg Fortress Publishers, 2008**

A view of the spiritual, intellectual, emotional, social and physical difficulties people face as they live with chronic illness and disabilities. Includes spiritual resources, emotional supports, intellectual answers and practical solutions for people with illness.

Caring Connections: www.caringinfo.org

A program of the National Hospice and Palliative Care Organization (NHPCO), this consumer and community initiative aims to improve care for people living with serious illness, end of life and grief. Provides free resources and information to help people learn about a wide range of issues, including illness and caregiving.

Handbook for Mortals: Guidance for People Facing Serious Illness, **by Joanne Lynn and Joan Harrold; Oxford University Press, 2001**

Helps individuals trust their own feelings and values and use them—to live with serious illness, learn what to expect, find meaning and ways to cope with loss and manage pain and other symptoms. Includes disease-specific information, guidance on end of life decisions and resource lists.

Healing and the Jewish Imagination; Spiritual and Practical Perspectives on Judaism and Health, **edited by William Cutter; Jewish Lights Publishing, 2008**

Explores the Jewish tradition for providing comfort in times of illness and spiritual perspectives for suffering. Scholars, teachers, artists and activists examine the aspects of mortality and the distinction between curing and healing.

Kitchen Table Wisdom: Stories That Heal, **by Rachel Naomi Remen; Riverhead Books, 1996**

Stories of patients who have faced illness and developed new ways to understand suffering, strength and peace of mind as well as stories of physicians experiencing new ways to care for patients.

Living With Life-Threatening Illness: A Guide for Patients, Their Families, & Caregivers, **by Kenneth J. Doka; Jossey-Bass Publishers, 1998**

Hands-on guide for patients, families, and caregivers on how to live an affirming existence while facing the physical and spiritual traumas of life-threatening illness.

National Center for Jewish Healing: www.ncjh.org

Helps communities meet the spiritual needs of Jews living with illness, loss and other significant life challenges. Offers consultation, resource material, publications, training and referrals to community resources.

National Institute on Aging: www.nia.nih.gov

Offers a selection of free publications on a wide variety of subjects including conditions and diseases, choosing medical care, medication, making sense of health care information and communication with health care providers.

Talking to Alzheimer's: Simple Ways to Connect When You Visit With a Family Member or Friend, **by Claudia J. Strauss; New Harbinger Publications, Inc., 2002**

Tools for effective, meaningful and mutually rewarding communication with a family member or friend who has Alzheimer's Disease.

You Are One of Us: Successful Clergy/Church Connections to Alzheimer's Families, **by Lisa P. Gwyther; Duke University Medical Center, 1995**

A booklet for churches and clergy that explains Alzheimer's disease, how to communicate with those who have it and how it affects families. Also a guide for tending to the spiritual self and ways of reaching out to those with Alzheimer's and their families.

Living With Caregiving

While many people do not identify themselves as caregivers, one American in five provides care for another adult, often a family member. There are currently an estimated 44 million caregivers in the United States—and according to the U.S. Census Bureau, that number is expected to surge as today's baby boomers age.

The care currently provided occurs in a number of ways.

Care at home. For many family caregivers, providing care at home involves:

- administering and tracking medications

- assisting with physical care, such as changing dressings or skin care

- helping with activities of daily living, such as eating, dressing and toileting

- assisting with practical matters such as transportation, running errands and cooking, and

- offering emotional and spiritual support as the person they care for lives with illness.

Long-distance care. In today's mobile society, an increasing number of family members provide long-distance care. Some caregivers who do not live close enough to provide care directly may research and direct onsite caregiving services, find a local point person, organization or facility to help direct care and check in or visit periodically to ensure care is occurring. Long-distance caregivers may also work closely with physicians and other care providers by phone or email.

Whether providing hands-on or long-distance caregiving, all caregivers may experience significant challenges.

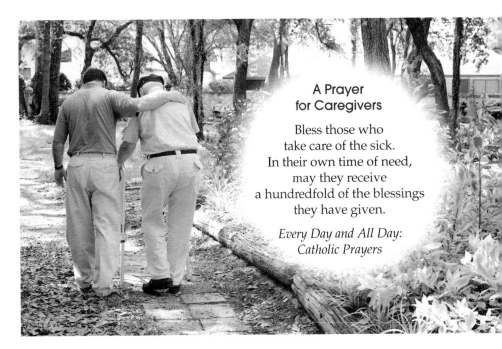

A Prayer for Caregivers

Bless those who take care of the sick. In their own time of need, may they receive a hundredfold of the blessings they have given.

Every Day and All Day: Catholic Prayers

Challenges of Caregiving

Much of the family caregiving provided today is informal, unsupported and unfunded by health and social systems. As the level of caregiving increases, the challenges also increase. One-third of family caregivers, the ones who deliver the most intense levels of care, are at greatest risk of compromising their own well-being: physically, psychologically, financially—and spiritually.

Physical stress. Studies show that caregivers are less healthy than those not involved in caring for others. In general, caregivers are more like to have a decreased immunity to illness, higher hospitalization rates, higher incidence of headaches, insomnia and heart disease and higher death rates.

Psychological toll. Caregivers experience high rates of depression, anxiety, stress, guilt and suicide. And caregiver stress and exhaustion can develop into anger, social withdrawal, irritability, inability to concentrate, problems at work and alcohol and drug abuse.

Financial strain. Outside sources such as Medicare, Medicaid and private insurance do little to cover caregiving costs, often causing family members to use their savings or to cut back on their own health care expenses to help cover costs. Long-term care insurance may cover some costs, but also can be expensive and difficult to understand. In addition, more than 35% of caregivers quit their jobs or reduce workhours because of family caregiving; four in ten go into poverty while providing care. Caregivers with increased financial burden may experience added anxiety, sleeping difficulties, depression and new or worsening health problems.

Spiritual challenges. Caregivers may have deep questions raised by the experiences of illness and caregiving that affect their faith. They may question why their loved one is coping with a difficult illness and why their own burden is so intense. They may become angry at or feel abandoned by God. They may experience guilt for things they did or did not do—or for not remaining as active in their faith community.

The Opportunities of Caregiving

Along with challenges, caregivers may experience growth through their experiences. As family members or friends navigate illness with others living with illness, they may develop new strengths and learn new skills to:

- provide hands-on care for another person, perhaps for the first time

- offer emotional support and reassurance for someone they love living with illness

- access health benefits or advocate for a loved one in the medical system

- tap into social networks to find assistance support, and

- discover spiritual strengths and grow into a deeper faith.

As an illness changes, the knowledge, skills and daily life of caregivers will need to change as well. Just as illness is a journey for the person living with it, it is also a journey for family and friends who are providing care.

Resources for Specific Faith Traditions and Cultures

As a complement to the resources listed in this toolkit, the Duke Institute on Care at the End of Life offers an online guide to resources that specific denominations and faith traditions have developed for supporting people living with serious illness, caregiving, end of life and grief. Includes resources for working with diverse populations such as African Americans, Latinos and Chinese-Americans and for working across cultures and in interfaith settings. Available at www.iceol.duke.edu.

Additional Resources on Caregiving

***And Thou Shalt Honor: The Caregiver's Companion*, edited by Beth Witrogen McLeod; Rodale, Inc., 2003**

Information on caregiving—including managing day-to-day tasks, accessing public and private resources, navigating the legal and financial maze, assembling a support network, understanding the changing family dynamics and surviving and thriving in the caregiver role.

***Caregiving: The Spiritual Journey of Love, Loss, and Renewal*, by Beth Witroge McLeod; Wiley, 2000**

Framed by the author's personal experience as a caregiver and informed by the tales of others, this book explores medical and financial problems, all aspects of spirituality and such issues as depression, stress, housing, home care and end of life concerns.

Caring.com

Created to help adult children care for aging parents and other loved ones. This website provides practical information, easy-to-use tools, and personal support by experts in geriatric medicine, legal matters, finances, housing and family issues, as well as community support from caregivers.

***The Complete Bedside Companion: No-Nonsense Advice on Caring for the Seriously Ill*, by Rodger McFarlane and Philip Bashe; Fireside, 1999**

Information and resources to help respond to the challenges of caring for a person who is seriously ill or dying. Outlines practical skills necessary for caregivers, provides guidance in creating a day-to-day care plan, describes diseases, offers tips unique to each illness and offers strategic guidance to enable caregivers to advocate effectively.

Elderweb: www.elderweb.com

Extensive resource for information on eldercare as well as legal, financial and public policies concerning the elderly. Provides a state-by-state link to long-term care, as well as a library of articles, reports, news and events.

Family Caregiver Alliance: www.caregiver.org

Provides caregiving information and advice, factsheets and publications, newsletters, groups and information about public policy and research.

***So Far Away: Twenty Questions for Long-Distance Caregivers*, by the National Institute on Aging; 2006**

Offers tips on caring for an older relative, family friend or former neighbor. Organized in a question/answer format with a resource list at the end. Up to 25 free copies available at www.nia.nih.gov.

U.S. Administration on Aging's Eldercare Locator: www.elderweb.com

This public service of the U.S. Administration on Aging links those who need assistance with state and local area agencies on aging and community-based organizations that serve older adults and their caregivers.

***With Sweetness From the Rock: A Jewish Spiritual Companion for Caregivers*, by Stephanie Dickstein; National Center for Jewish Healing**

A companion for caregivers—offering spiritual support drawn from Jewish tradition, ancient and modern texts and the experience of others.

> We're a nation of caregivers. Everybody has a caregiver story to tell.
>
> Elinor Ginzler,
> *AARP Director for
> Livable Communities*

Creating Unbroken Circles Around Illness

Begin with the chapter "Creating Unbroken Circles of Care" to explore strategies to address leadership development, education, congregational care, worship, communications and supportive and accessible space. After doing the exercises there and learning about models for ministry and exploring resources, you will be ready to incorporate the following season-specific information on education, congregational care and worship for people living with illness.

Illness Education

As you identify key topics for education around illness, use the ideas and resources offered in this section of the toolkit as a starting place.

Some potential ideas for educational sessions related to serious illness include:

- Coping With Pain and Suffering
- Dealing With a Diagnosis: What to Expect
- Understanding Alzheimer's and Dementia
- Effective Communication With Professional Caregivers During Illness, and
- Helping Children Understand Illness.

As explained in more detail in the earlier chapter, "Creating Unbroken Circles of Care," education that features interactive adult learning is most helpful. (For a sample educational session, see "Spiritual Support for Family and Friends," below.)

Educational Sessions

Whether you offer education sessions about serious illness during a designated adult education time such as Sunday School, or create a time such as a weekday evening program, you may use or adapt the following model sessions. They may be used as written or adapted. As you plan additional sessions, they offer a format you can use for other related topics.

---

1   Educational Session 1: Spiritual Support for Family and Friends

---

People who are very ill often ask spiritual questions—seeking comfort, meaning and hope. While clergy, chaplains and other spiritual leaders may play important roles in spiritual care, family and friends can offer important spiritual support, too. This session explores the spiritual impact of illness and discusses ways to support ourselves and others through it.

1. Opening: 5 minutes

Select a scripture, poem or quote or offer a prayer to begin. You may use one of devotional resources listed in this toolkit or choose your own.

2. Exploring Your Beliefs About Illness: 15 minutes

Begin by asking participants to work in pairs or small groups to remember a time when they experienced an illness, a significant life transition or loss.

Ask them to consider the following questions:

- How did that experience affect you spiritually?

Materials for the Session

"Offering Spiritual Support for Family or Friends" handout from Caring Connections, by James L. Brooks. Printed versions are available in bulk at www.nhpco.org.

- How did your spirituality affect the experience?
- What spiritual strengths did you discover?
- What questions or concerns did you have?

Remind participants that even within families, among friends and in faith communities, spiritual beliefs and experiences may be very different—but their own views may color their perceptions of others' experiences. An openness to listen with respect is vital in supporting others through illness. If time allows, invite a few participants to share key insights from their small group interaction.

3. Spiritual Issues During Illness: 15 minutes

People who are very ill often draw on their spiritual beliefs as a source of strength. However, facing illness may also bring up a wide range of thoughts, emotions and questions.

Use the overview of serious illness in this chapter of the toolkit to discuss possible issues people living with illness may confront, such as:

- questioning meaning and purpose
- dealing with guilt and forgiveness
- experiencing a loss of faith, and
- facing questions about faith tradition or faith community.

Ask participants to discuss these questions, using prompts such as:

- Are there spiritual issues that surprise you?
- Are there any that make you uncomfortable?
- Are there spiritual issues you think others have an especially hard time facing?

- Are there any key issues that you find missing here?

Remind participants that having questions about spirituality is a normal part of dealing with an illness. Rather than trying to answer such questions, you become a "spiritual companion" when you support others in asking them. Reinforce the idea that these spiritual reactions do not necessarily indicate a loss of faith but rather a quest for meaning and an experience of change and growth.

4. Offering Spiritual Support for Family and Friends: 10 minutes

One of the most important things friends and family members can do for people living with illness is to know how to meet them in their spiritual journeys with illness and to offer support. However, many are unsure how to help. As you prepare participants in your session, briefly review the following tips people can use to prepare themselves for visiting with persons who are ill. If you have copies of the handout "Offering Spiritual Support for Family and Friends," distribute them at this time.

Teach the following tips for offering spiritual support during visits with others who are ill. Offer brief stories or examples that help bring the tips to life or ask participants if they have a story or examples to share. For example, when discussing clichés, you may ask if participants have ever heard or said clichés about illness they realized were not helpful. Simple follow up questions such as "Tell me more about that" can deepen the discussion.

5. Small Group Discussion: 10 minutes

After you teach the tips for offering spiritual support, ask participants to return to their pairs or small groups to discuss to following questions.

- What do you think matters most in providing spiritual support for others?

TIPS FOR OFFERING SPIRITUAL SUPPORT WHILE VISITING THE ILL

When offering spiritual support for someone living with illness, be sensitive to the following tips:

Be mindful of the setting. Find a quiet time and place to begin a conversation about spiritual matters.

Ask permission to have the conversation. People cope with illness in different ways at different times, so begin by saying something such as: "I was wondering if you might want to talk with me about how your illness is affecting you spiritually."

Be present. Fear of not knowing what to say keeps many people from having spiritual conversations with people who are very ill. Realize that it is your presence that matters most.

Ask open, supportive questions. Give the person who is ill a chance to lead in the conversation to discuss his or her own questions, strengths and concerns.

Listen with an open heart. Because many thoughts, emotions and questions are possible, the only way to understand where the ill person is spiritually is to listen.

Be open to the emotions that may come up. People who are ill may express sadness, anger, guilt, denial, hope, joy, peace and relief. Those expressions may be a way to seek healing or peace.

Avoid clichés. Responses such as "It's part of God's plan" or "Everything happens for a reason" often short-circuit conversation rather than encouraging it. Listen for the thoughts and feeling in the questions.

Offer compassionate support. Keep your focus on the other person: his or her stories, questions, thoughts and feelings. Express your support, encouragement or love as the person faces these issues.

Use spiritual resources as appropriate. Based on your experience with the person, offer fitting prayer, spiritual readings, music or rituals. Ask if the person has a favorite prayer, scripture, reading, hymn or sacred psalm he or she would like to read, hear or sing together.

Remember that you are not in this alone. As a friend or family member, know your comfort zones and your limits. Encourage the involvement of professional clergy, chaplains or other spiritual leaders with expertise in spiritual care when possible.

And a reminder that bears repeating: Respect the fact that each person deals with spiritual issues in an individual time and way. Another person's timetable may not be your timetable, so be patient.

- What part of providing spiritual support is most challenging for you?

- What has your own experience taught you about how your faith community can support members through illness?

- What can our faith community do to support people spiritually through illness?

Use the insights you gain from this discussion to help inform your congregational care planning.

6. Closing: 5 minutes

You may choose to close with a prayer or a reading or by offering participants the opportunity to spontaneously offer a word of hope, a meditation or an intention.

2   Educational Session 2: Becoming a Patient Advocate

Today's health care is complicated, technical and splintered. The traditional approach to health care suggests that sick patients enter the system and their only jobs are to rest and regain their health. Because of the current state of medical care, this is no longer possible. In fact, the greatest irony of illness often is that when one is at their worst is precisely when they need to be at their best.

A patient or a patient's advocate must take responsibility for understanding the illnesses and options involved, communicating with health care providers and keeping a close eye on what is being done so that they can act before mistakes are made. Being a proactive patient advocate takes skills, practice—and most of all, a clear understanding of the need.

1. Opening: 5 minutes

Begin with a reading or prayer. Then ask one or two participants to briefly describe an experience they have had in the health care system that required them to speak up for themselves or another person. Stress the importance of learning about patient advocacy.

2. Advocacy as a Spiritual Practice: 15 minutes

While patient advocacy is often seen as a recent development in health care, in reality, health care advocacy is an ancient practice.

Materials for the Session

"Three Keys to Patient Advocacy" by Tiffany Christensen, page 39 of this toolkit.

Hebrew and Christian scriptures illustrate two different aspects of patient advocacy.

Practical advocacy. When someone is sick, even the simplest things become difficult. Being a practical advocate means taking responsibility for the seemingly small aspects of life that most of us take for granted. Examples may include collecting patients' mail, driving them to doctor's appointments, bringing them groceries or preparing their meals.

In Hebrew scripture 1 Kings 17:8-24, the impoverished widow Zarephath was caring for her very ill son. When God sent the prophet Elijah to her doorstep, the prophet asked

for food and water. Because she generously responded, despite her own hardship, she was rewarded with an undiminished supply. This mother acted as a practical advocate, giving her son the life-sustaining nourishment he needed.

In the Christian gospel Luke 5:17-20, several men carried their sick friend to be healed by Jesus, but the crowd was too thick to reach him. Instead of giving up, the men carried their friend to the roof, cut a hole in the tiles and lowered the bed through the ceiling at Jesus' feet. Through their creative and proactive practical advocacy, their friend was healed.

After sharing one of these stories of practical advocacy or a another one you select, ask participants to briefly discuss ways they can imagine being a practical advocate for themselves or others—in pairs, small groups or one large group.

Emotional and spiritual patient advocacy. When someone copes with physical symptoms of illness, the emotional and spiritual symptoms can be equally challenging. In a typical health care setting, it is not unusual for the emotional and spiritual self to be ignored. As a patient, friend or family member, it is important to advocate not only for good physical care but for good emotional and spiritual care as well. This might mean actively listening to a person as they cry, vent anger or raise spiritual questions or lament. It may mean helping them secure access to a counselor or therapist.

In some cases, patients might be facing misdiagnosis or misunderstandings and be forced to contradict doctors, psychiatrists or insurance companies. An advocate can support them emotionally through these issues. This type of scenario requires significant emotional steadiness on the part of the patients and their advocates. This necessity echoes the well-known story of Job in Hebrew scripture. Job was tormented by those who inaccurately interpreted events and falsely "diagnosed" him as being outside of God's graces. In Job's story, he fought these misconceptions alone, never wavering on what he knew to be true. Job was his own emotional advocate.

After teaching about emotional and spiritual advocacy, ask participants to briefly discuss ways they can imagine being an emotional and spiritual advocate for themselves or others. The discussion may occur in pairs, small groups or one large group.

3. Putting Patient Advocacy Into Practice: 35 minutes

When most of us think of patient advocacy, we think about medical advocacy. In medical advocacy situations, patients and family members work to ensure the patient gets the best care possible by:

• being knowledgeable about the health problem

• being aware of what is being done to the patient, and

• asserting boundaries when necessary to preserve the health of the patient.

It is sometimes difficult to act in the moment, even for the most experienced patient advocate.

By following three simple steps, it is possible to practice being an advocate, even in very confusing situations.

The three steps to putting patient advocacy into practice are:

1. Stop or slow down the situation or conversation.

2. State your concerns and ask for clarity.

3. Propose your solution.

Cluster participants into groups of three to six people to discuss medical patient advocacy situations. The groups can use a real-life situation that happened to one of the participants or to one of their family members or friends. Encourage them to pick scenarios that are not extremely complicated. They should be something that can be reasonably resolved in one conversation.

Examples:

1. You are in the hospital and a young resident you have never met before comes into your room. He tells you he wants to dramatically change your medications based on the morning's blood work. You have been on the same medications for a long time without any problems and you worry that changing

> *Often, we have to go to extremes of doing too much or too little for someone before we can find the "right extent" of helping.*
>
> Wendy Lustbader,
> *Counting on Kindness*

them could be detrimental to your health. How do you advocate for yourself?

2. Your family member had hip surgery approximately one month ago. Tonight, the person suddenly collapsed and was transported to the emergency room. Now in the ER, the doctor does not seem concerned and wants to send your family member home with some oral antibiotics. This makes you feel very uncomfortable because you suspect something is wrong. You believe your family member should be monitored overnight. How do you advocate in this situation?

Ask each group to write out a loosely scripted scene for the story using the three steps for putting patient advocacy into practice. To make their brainstorming more real, the group may designate one participant to play the role of the professional and other participants to play the patient and others. After 15 minutes, ask the groups to read or act out their script as time allows. Ask all participants to discuss the ways each group demonstrated effective advocacy in their roleplay.

5. Closing: 5 minutes

You may choose to close with a prayer, a reading or by offering participants the opportunity to spontaneously offer a word of hope, a meditation or an intention.

This teaching session was contributed by Tiffany Christensen, www. sickgirlspeaks.com. The two teaching sessions above are excerpted from Engaging With Compassion: Educational Sessions for Congregations Around Illness, End of Life and Grief, *by James L. Brooks, available from Project Compassion: www.project-compassion.org.*

An Illness Series

While offering a single educational session can be effective, a series gives you the opportunity to explore the topic at hand more fully. During the course of a year, you may offer a series of five or six sessions, each focusing on a different topic or you may opt to conduct a retreat that covers a series of topics.

It may be beneficial to solicit the help of professionals in your community such as doctors, faith community nurses, hospital chaplains, hospice social workers or specialists in children's issues, as well as congregation members who have experienced illness or caregiving to help develop and lead the series.

Be sure to include discussions of the spiritual, emotional and social implications of the illness and to incorporate participants' experiences. If you wish, you may time the session to coincide with the calendar of health observance. (See Creating Unbroken Circles of Care, page 21, for more on this.)

Ideas for series concerning illness are offered below.

- Understanding Illness Series. Possible topics include:
  - Understanding Pain and Pain Management
  - Understanding Cancer
  - Understanding Alzheimer's and Dementia
  - Understanding Heart Disease, and
  - Understanding How to Advocate for Yourself or Another Person.
- The Spiritual Journey of Illness Series. Topics might include:
  - The Spiritual Experience of Illness
  - Suffering and Hope: The Search for Meaning During Illness
  - Exploring What Healing Means During Illness
  - Family Stories: Creative Ways to Share Stories and Memories, and
  - Caregiving as a Spiritual Journey.

As you offer educational sessions, be sure to ask participants for feedback, either verbally or on an evaluation form, to find out what they found most helpful about the session and what topics they would be interested in exploring in future sessions or series.

Additional Resources on Education

***Christian Caregiving: A Way of Life*, by Kenneth Haugk; Augsburg Fortress Publishing, 1994**

Helps congregations teach their members the basics of Christian caring and daily caregiving. The course may be structured as a series of weekly meetings or a daylong or weekend retreat.

***Engaging With Compassion: Educational Sessions for Congregations Around Illness, End of Life and Grief*, by James L. Brooks; Project Compassion Press, 2008**

An educational curriculum offering interactive adult education sessions around illness and caregiving as well as end of life and grief. All sessions can be adapted for many different congregational sessions. Includes key teaching tips and resources for facilitators. Available at www.project-compassion.org.

***Stories: The Family Legacy*, by Richard Stone; StoryWork Institute Press, 2004**

Practical, creative strategies and ideas to help people tell their own stories that can be used by individuals, families or communities. Can be a resource and idea book for planning education and offering congregational care. Available in individual copies or in bulk at www.storywork.com.

***When Bad Things Happen to Good People*, by Harold S. Kushner; Anchor, 2004**

Reprises the author's experience when his teenage son died, particularly the struggle with the question: Where do we find the resources to cope when tragedy strikes? Can be the basis of discussion groups or offer helpful illustrations for educational sessions.

Congregational Care

The following congregational care models, tools, tips and stories offered to support people living with illness complement the more general congregational care materials and resources in the chapter, Creating Unbroken Circles of Care. After doing the exercises, learning about models for ministry and exploring resources in that chapter, consider the following models specifically for people living with illness.

Visiting the Sick

Bikur Cholim, or "visiting the sick," is a Hebrew term encompassing a wide range of activities performed by an individual or a group to provide comfort and support to people who are ill, homebound, isolated or otherwise in distress. Resources specific to Jewish congregations include laws of Bikur Cholim, prayers for visitors and guidelines for establishing synagogue groups. However, many of the principles and guidelines are helpful for all faith communities.

Called to Care

Called to Care is a resource designed to equip congregational caregivers for ministries of visitation, support and community service. Accompanying the notebook are Carecards, with information on 52 topics, including death and dying and catastrophic illness. The series has been used successfully by congregations of all sizes. Small to medium-size congregations have found this resource particularly helpful and affordable.

The complete Called to Care notebook is available from United Church of Christ Resources by calling 800-537-3394 or through the

CONVERSATION ESSENTIALS FOR VISITING THE SICK

Visiting is an investment of time and includes attention, patience, perceptive listening, sincere concern, openness and communication skills.

As in all verbal communication, tone of voice is very important and can change the meaning behind the question.

Below are techniques to help facilitate communication when making a visit or talking with the person on the phone:

OPEN-ENDED QUESTIONS

Use questions that elicit an in-depth response, ones that cannot be answered with "yes" or "no." Use "how" and "what" instead of "do," "did" and "were."

Examples:

Are you feeling upset right now? (Closed)

How do you feel right now? (Open)

Do you like to read? (Closed)

What are some activities that you enjoy doing? (Open)

Open-ended questions are good conversation starters:

What was it like growing up in the 1930s (or other date)?

How is your family doing?

What do you think about____?

Help the person expand

"Tell me more..."

"Tell me about it..."

"You seem upset..."

Ask questions to better understand

"I'm not sure I really know what you mean when you say..."

"Let's go over that one more time."

Redirect the conversation

"Thank you for your concern, but I'd really like to hear about..."

"You mentioned before that..."

"Let's go back to..."

Review past and present efforts at problem solving

"Have you talked with anyone about this?"

"What do you usually do when...?"

"What have you done about this so far?"

"What choices do you feel you might have?"

SOURCE: WWW.BIKURCHOLIMCC.ORG.

'My Whole Community Stood With Me'

Elizabeth (Betsy) C. Eder is a Duke Divinity School student, a Presbyterian Church (USA) elder, and the former Triangle Area (NC) Stephen Ministry Network Co-ordinator. Here she tells how her faith community buoyed her up during a life-threatening illness.

Many of us think of death as something others suffer, but not something that we ourselves must face until we reach a very old age.

I was forced to face my own mortality 20 years ago at the age of 27. Though I had always lived a healthy, vigorous life, at the moment my first pregnancy was confirmed, I was diagnosed with a rare blood disorder. I was told that I could die of a stroke at any minute.

The doctors sent me home, not to furbish a nursery for my baby but to enter a kind of an advent sea-son, preparing for my own death or the death of my unborn child. I stood exposed and alone. Thank-fully, my child and I survived.

When I went through another health crisis a few years ago, this time I was blessed to be part of a loving faith community. During a worship service, I went for-ward, was anointed with oil, and received prayer for strength and healing and courage.

I also received prayers and spiritual support from my 20 fellow Stephen Ministers. I felt the strength of the community's prayers on my behalf and knew that should things get worse, I would not be alone. As a child of God, I felt that my whole com-munity stood with me.

website at www.unitedchurchpress.com. In addition, *Called to Care: A Pocket Handbook for Caregivers* is available to order or download free at www.ucc.org/ministers.

Faith in Action

This major national volunteer initiative launched interfaith volunteer caregiving programs across the United States from 1983 to 2008. While grants are no longer available, program development resources are available free on the website. Congregations interested in developing member support programs will also find downloadable information on program management, volunteer coordination and communication.

In addition to accessing the resources, you may find one of the 650 Faith in Action nonprofit programs operating in your area. Your congregation may be able to refer members for volunteer caregiving support. Your local Faith in Action organization may also be willing to partner with you to train and support volunteers, increasing your capacity.

For more information, go to www.fianationalnetwork.org.

Stephen Ministries

The Stephen Ministry series is a Christian model for training and organizing lay people to provide one-to-one spiritual care for people in and around your congregation. The Stephen Series provides the structure, training and resources to set up and administer lay caring ministry called "Stephen Ministry." In such congregations, lay caregivers—or Stephen Ministers—provide one-to-one care to the bereaved, hospitalized, terminally ill, separated, divorced,

unemployed, relocated and others facing a crisis or life challenge.

For more details, call 314-428-2600 or go to www.stephenministries.org.

A Team Approach

Faith communities across the country have successfully adopted team approaches as part of creating circles of care for members and their families living with illness.

One successful model, support teams, are groups of volunteer members organized to pool their talents and efforts to provide support—primarily for people living with illness, end of life and grief. (To learn more, see Creating Unbroken Circles of Care, pages 25 and 26.)

Support teams are a particularly successful, sustainable approach to creating support for people living with illness over time. Many such teams have provided consistent practical, emotional, spiritual and quality of life support for people living with illness for months or years. Because the effort is shared, volunteer members are less likely to burn out.

Support teams also have the added benefit of supporting family caregivers as well as the person living with illness, meeting a wider range of needs. While a team is not necessary for every situation in which people live with illness and caregiving, it is a powerful model when congregations want to mobilize helpful community around members.

Project Compassion: 'Magic Can Happen'

Since 2002, Project Compassion, the lead nonprofit organization in the Support Team Network has created more than 200 caregiving Support Teams with more than 1,500 community volunteers in Durham-Chapel Hill, NC in partnership with area faith communities and other organizations. Nationally, the organization has trained representatives of faith communities and other organizations from 42 states. Here is one of Project Compassion's experiences working with a faith community to create an unbroken circle of care and support.

On a warm spring evening, Sonia Norris finishes classes at the Duke Divinity School, picks up a large pizza and drives to Toni and James "Tinker" Turner's ranch-style home in northern Durham. The couple greets Norris at the door, puts the pizza in the oven and invites her back to the bedroom of their 20-year-old daughter, Elizabeth.

"Sonia always speaks to Elizabeth when she comes," says Toni, her voice filled with gratitude. "All the Support Team people do."

That team reflects the efforts of Norris, who brought together the Turners' faith community with Project Compassion, a national leader in the field of volunteer Support Teams.

The Turners adopted Elizabeth, their only child, as an infant. She was healthy until first grade, when she began having trouble seeing the blackboard. A referral from the family eye doctor led them to Duke Hospital and, ultimately, the diagnosis of Batten disease—a rare fatal inherited disorder of the nervous system that typically begins with vision loss and epileptic seizures. The disease, which is painless, gradually leads to progressive cognitive and physical loss with death usually resulting in the late teens to early 30s.

With help from Project Compassion, Norris organized a support care team for the Turners through Union Grove United Methodist Church in Hillsborough, where Tinker's family has worshiped for generations. At the first meeting, 20 volunteers showed up.

"Project Compassion's approach to care takes the burden off the individual," says Norris. "It's a shared responsibility, rather than any one person being overwhelmed. Some people love to cook, some just want to make deliveries. The model helps build relationships among the team members and it's not overwhelming at all."

The Support Team has provided a meal every other day for the past year, giving Toni and Tinker more time to spend with Elizabeth. "They really needed help," says Norris. "They've been providing her care for 24/7 for a long time."

With respite care from the team, the Turners recently went out alone—to the mall and to dinner—for the first time in 15 years.

"We sat down and I looked at Tinker and said, 'I don't know what to talk about,'" says Toni. "You know, you just forget what it's like to go out alone."

As Jeanne Twohig, Deputy Director of Duke's Institute on Care at the End of Life, says, "With a team approach, you can see how transformational this ministry can be. When everybody is bringing what they can to the table, magic can happen."

Adapted from "Building Bridges: A Student's Passion for Caring," by Elisabeth Stagg, originally printed in Divinity Magazine, a publication of Duke Divinity School, Spring 2006

Additional Resources on Support Teams

The Mitzvah of Bikur Cholim: A Model for Building Community in Contemporary Synagogues, **by Janet Offel**

Guide that offers an outline for synagogues on adopting team principles to Bikur Cholim groups. Free online at www. jewishhealing.org/downloads/seraf-MitzvahBC.pdf.

Share the Care: How to Organize a Group to Care for Someone Who Is Seriously Ill, **by Cappy Capossela and Sheila Warnock; Fireside, Inc., 2004**

Details common caregiving tasks, from major ones: checking someone into the hospital, sorting out insurance coverage, keeping track of medications, to the minor: walking the dog, preparing a meal, or just companionship. Describes a group approach that can turn a circle of people into a caregiver team.

Support Team Guidebook **by the Support Team Network, available from Project Compassion at 919-402-1844 or www.project-compassion.org**

Provides an overview of the team approach, steps for creating, orienting and supporting Support Teams as well as ready-to-use forms, tip sheets and stories.

As the lead organization in the Support Team Network, Project Compassion also offers **Support Team Development Conferences** to teach individuals and organizations how to organize and support a team approach. In addtion, the organization published *The Experience of Volunteer Caregiving* by Marilyn Hartman and James L. Brooks in 2008, a report on the first comparative research study of the effectiveness of the team approach in community-based volunteer caregiving. For a free copy of the study or more information about Support Team Leadership Development Conferences, contact Project Compassion at 919-402-1844 or go to www.project-compassion.org.

Support Groups

Support groups are a way for congregations to extend care and camaraderie, both to members who are ill and to those who care for them.

For those who are ill. Illness often isolates many people at a time when they need social support the most. Just as the absence of social support can lead to higher risks of illness and stress, strong social bonds can lead to healing and contribute to an increased sense of community.

Support groups are often informal groups of individuals with similar concerns that meet regularly to exchange information and provide peer support. The group leader may be a peer or a professional facilitator. Groups may be self-organized or part of a larger organization.

In many communities, disease-specific organizations such as the Alzheimer's Association or the American Cancer Society offer ongoing support groups. Many lesser-known organizations offer groups as well. Check out the possibilities in your area and connect members with local chapters and groups that fit their needs.

An additional step congregations can take is to partner with a disease-specific organization or other nonprofit to host or facilitate a support group. This can make the group more accessible for faith community members and help raise awareness of the need for support within the congregation.

A faith community may also opt to create a support group of it is own, either restricted to its members or open to the community. For example, one congregation recently began a peer-to-peer support group for members living with chronic illness. These members, who have a variety of illnesses but often deal with similar situations and struggles, come together twice a month to discuss their challenges and concerns.

One of the clergy members facilitates the meetings and weaves in spiritual components, and the faith community nurse organizes guest speakers to offer information about particular topics the group members decide they would like addressed. At one monthly meeting, the group learned about assistive devices. Another month, they learned about new issues related to Medicare and long-term care planning. The next month, they walked a small labyrinth and shared their experiences.

By coming together to support one another, these members have the opportunity to feel connected, share their experiences with others and feel the support of the faith community as they deal with their illnesses.

For caregivers. Some congregations also offer support groups for caregivers. One congregation in Minneapolis, Minnesota, hosts such a support group that meets once a month over lunch. Facilitated and coordinated by a trained lay leader, this group opens with a reading of scripture and a devotional about caregiving and then continues with five minutes of silence, which caregivers report is a welcome moment of peace in their lives.

The group addresses different topics each week, including how to communicate with a loved one who is ill, caregiver stress, long-distance caregiving, tips for self-care and available resources for caregivers. During the meetings, the faith community provides lunch and volunteers who offer respite for the caregivers by going out to the homes and sitting with the caregivers' loved ones.

This enables the caregivers to have a change of scenery, a lunch and to take in a sense of community and spiritual support from their congregation, along with peace of mind that their loved ones are receiving good care.

Casa de Vida: Respite From Constant Caregiving

An outreach ministry of NorthPark Presbyterian Church, Dallas, Texas, Casa de Vida is weekly respite program for those who care for others with early onset Alzheimer's or related dementia being cared for at home.

For four hours every Tuesday, a number of local residents come to the church to engage in life-enhancing activities such as music, art, exercise, games and crafts. The day ends with lunch. Each participant is assigned a Faith Companion. These volunteers are assigned to participants, reassuring them and providing a sense of weekly continuity. Once a month, NorthPark Presbyterian pastors conduct a short worship and communion service.

While participants are at Casa de Vida, their caregivers—many of whom struggle alone through the 24-hour task of providing care—have the opportunity to run errands, visit friends, shop or go home for quiet time. Through Casa de Vida, NorthPark Presbyterian helps create its own unbroken circle of care and support for people living with early onset Alzheimer's or dementia and their caregivers.

For more information, go to www.northparkpres.org

Adult Day Programs

People living with illness often benefit from stimulation and a break from monotony. And family caregivers also often need a break from the stress and constancy of offering care. While hired assistance and private day care programs can be options for some people, they are simply too expensive for others.

To bridge this gap, some faith communities have developed affordable adult day programs, often operating out of their own facilities. These programs may be designed specifically for adults with memory disorders such as Alzheimer's disease and dementia or open to all adults who require a certain level of assistance. The programs may be offered daily, weekly, biweekly or monthly and they may last a few hours or all day.

Developing and supporting an adult day program requires appropriate resources, infrastructure and protocols, all of which differ by locale. For more information about adult day programs, contact the National Adult Day Services Association, Inc. at 877-745-1440 or go to www.nadsa.org.

Creative Support Ministries

Some congregations tap into members' interests in the creative arts as a way to extend care and support. Below are a few examples—helpful for faith communities new to creative expression and those seeking ideas to refresh ongoing ministries.

Music Ministries

Music can provide meaningful ways to commune with God, feel comforted and connect with the communities of faith. Recognizing this power, many faith communities offer music as part of congregational care. For example, some Christian congregations do not wait until the Christmas season to carol for members living with illness or caregiving. Small vocal or instrumental ensembles or musical support teams may take sacred music to the homes of members every month or quarter.

Some congregations create CDs for members to play when they would like to hear the voices or sounds of their community. Such CDs can include messages, wishes or prayers that address the intended recipient by name.

Prayer for Healing

In the beginning, creating God,
you formed my being.

You knit me together
in my mother's womb.

To my flesh and blood
you gave the breath of life.

O loving One,
renew me this day in your love.

Grant me life
as a gift of your faithfulness.

Grant me light to journey by.

Grant me hope to sustain me.

May this mantle be for me
a sign of your healing presence

May it warm me
when I am cold and weary.

May it surround me
with comfort when I am suffering.

O Christ who healed the broken
in body and spirit,

Be with me
and all that suffer this day.

Be with the doctors, nurses,
technicians, chaplains

And all that care for the sick.

Be with the families
and friends of those

Abiding with and
comforting the sick.

May your gentle, yet strong touch
reach out to heal all the

Broken and hurting people and
places in the world.

Amen.

SOURCE: THE PRAYER SHAWL MINISTRY OF
THE UNITED CHURCH OF CHAPEL HILL (UCC);
CHAPEL HILL, NORTH CAROLINA

Prayer Shawls and Throws

Some congregations create handmade prayer shawls—also called comfort shawls, peace shawls or mantles—to show love and support to members who are ill. Others make quilts or knit or crochet throws for warmth and comfort. The crafters may gather regularly and work as a group or work on the item alone at home. Often, the person making the shawl, lap blanket or throw offers prayers and blessings for the recipient while creating it. After the piece is completed, it may be blessed by the maker, by a prayer group or by the congregation during a worship service.

When the completed item is delivered to the recipient, it is often accompanied by a letter or prayer, such as the Prayer for Healing offered here, that expresses its significance.

Prayer Quilt Ministries

Prayer Quilt Ministries offer a variation in how prayer shawls and quilts are made. Members of the congregation are invited to participate in tying the knots that hold the pieces of fabric together. As people tie each knot, they say a prayer for the recipient—and the recipient recognizes that each knot represents a prayer offered. Some faith communities incorporate this practice into regular worship services.

Additional Resources on Creative Ministries

Knitting Into the Mystery: A Guide to the Shawl-Knitting Ministry, by Susan S. Izard and Susan S. Jorgensen; Morehouse Publishing, 2003

Includes directions for knitting shawls and for starting a parish or community knitting ministry. Also includes stories and a selection of prayers, written from many faith traditions, to offer along with each completed shawl.

The Prayer Shawl Companion: 38 Knitted Designs to Embrace, Inspire and Celebrate Life, by Janet Bristow and Victoria Cole-Galo; Taunton, 2008

Offering wraps for all occasions, from baptism to remembrance, this book includes easy, intermediate and challenging patterns. Includes guidance on creating a peaceful, creative knitting environment and tells stories from both knitters and recipients.

Prayer Shawl Ministry: www.shawlministry.com

Website offering shawl instructions, prayers, meanings behind the shawl, tips and patterns, brochures, stories, news, photos and links.

Prayers & Squares: www.prayerquilt.org

An interfaith organization that offers instruction, patterns, conferences and resources to help congregations combine prayer with hand-tied quilts.

In another variation, quilters gather handwritten prayers that have been written for the recipient, then transfer and print these images directly onto fabric, which they gather and piece together into a quilt. Because the prayers are permanently incorporated into the quilt, recipients can repeatedly read the prayers offered for them.

While these quilts may be meaningful during times of illness, they can take on added meaning following a death, during times of grief. As grieving people use the prayer quilts that were made for their loved ones and as they read the prayers from the community, they can wrap themselves in a sign of the congregation's support.

> *The denial of suffering is, in fact, a better definition of illness than its acceptance.*
>
> M. Scott Peck,
> *The Road Less Traveled*

Additional Resources on Spiritual and Pastoral Care

The Art of Being a Healing Presence, by James E. Miller; Willowgreen Publishers, 2001

Offers seven steps to cultivating a healing presence: opening oneself, making the intention, preparing a space, honoring the other, offering what you have to give, receiving the gifts that come and living a life of wholeness and balance.

Cultivating Wholeness: A Guide to Care and Counseling in Faith Communities, by Margaret Zipse Kornfeld; Continuum International Publishing Group, 2000

A broad and thorough discussion of key issues that leaders of faith communities and lay caregivers regularly face. The material can be adapted either for brief periods of personal study or a focused continuing education piece for Stephen Ministers, deacons or clergy discussion groups.

Finding a Sacred Oasis in Illness: A Resource Manual for Clergy and Lay Visitation, by Steven L. Jeffers; Leathers Publishing, 2001

Covers a range of pastoral care issues from understanding the hospital experience from a patient's perspective, to strategies for pastoral care in a hospital setting to prayers for many hospital situations. Focused on offering practical and spiritual resources, accessible for both clergy and lay leaders.

Healing of Soul, Healing of Body: Spiritual Leaders Unfold the Strength and Solace in Psalms, edited by Simkha Y. Weintraub; Jewish Lights Publishing, 1994

Psalms and the inspiring commentaries that accompany them offer an anchor of spiritual support for those who are facing illness, as well as those who care for them. A resource for structuring educational sessions that integrate the psalms with illness and caregiving.

The Indispensable Guide to Pastoral Care, by Sharyl B. Peterson; Pilgrim Press, 2008

Includes a basic description of theological and practical dimensions of pastoral care, helps readers explore basic concepts in pastoral care students, including during times of illness and grief and demonstrates how to use traditional and contemporary resources to improve the care. Fit for clergy, students and lay leaders.

Jewish Pastoral Care: A Practical Handbook From Traditional and Contemporary Sources, edited by Dayle A. Friedman; Jewish Lights Publishing, 2005

A comprehensive reference for rabbis, cantors and laypeople who spiritually accompany those encountering joy, sorrow and change. This volume draws upon both Jewish tradition and the classical foundations of pastoral care to provide guidance.

Jewish Paths Toward Healing and Wholeness: A Personal Guide to Dealing With Suffering, by Kerry M. Olitzky; Jewish Lights Publishing, 2000

Combines the wisdom of Jewish tradition and insight from the author's personal experience and from dealing with the illness and pain of other people to show that healing the soul is vital for healing the body.

Pastoral Care: An Essential Guide, by John Patton; Abingdon Press, 2005

Concise reflection on what it means to offer guidance, reconciliation, healing, sustaining presence and empowerment to people in times of need and transition.

Sharing the Journey: Spiritual Assessment and Pastoral Response to Persons With Incurable Illnesses, by Cornelius J. Van Der Poel; Liturgical Press, 1998

Offers insight into the psychological and spiritual needs of people with incurable diseases and discusses spirituality as an integral dimension of human existence. Suggests ways to evaluate patients' needs and offers guidelines on accompanying on their journeys.

Spiritual Care: A Guide for Caregivers, by Judith Allen Shelly; InterVarsity Press, 2000

Deals with the issues that caregivers confront from a Christian perspective and discusses how to offer spiritual support to those facing suffering, illness or other crises. Also describes and evaluates alternative therapies popular in the health care and counseling fields.

Caring for Children and Teens

People of all ages face a range of difficult emotions and often ask tough questions when someone they care about is facing a serious illness. But for children, dealing with a serious illness can be particularly unsettling and confusing.

Children's needs are often overlooked when there is serious illness in the family—or when it is the child who faces the serious illness. People may assume children do not understand what's happening. And family members may not realize the impact the illness has on children of all ages. And some family members may try to shield children from difficult news or the realities of illness.

How Faith Communities Can Help

A significant step clergy and members can take is to ask specifically about how each child affected is coping. This will raise the awareness of parents and other family members that illness has an effect on younger members. It also reassures them that the faith community cares.

It is helpful for clergy and congregational caregivers to understand these children's needs. In addition to asking them about their feelings, clergy and lay leaders should be aware that children may need:

- accurate information about the illness in clear and concrete language

- an understanding of what causes the disease if that is known and how the disease is or is not spread

- assurance that they said, did or wished did not cause the disease or make it worse

- an understanding of the prognosis

- permission to ask questions and express feelings

- spiritual or pastoral support for spiritual questions and beliefs

- validation of their thoughts and feelings, and

- permission to keep on being a child.

Clergy and lay leaders can take the lead in talking with parents and other family members about the affected children's needs. They can work with parents using these tips to help provide support.

As challenging as serious illness is for children, it can also be an opportunity for growth and learning. With this in mind, pay special attention to a child's responses to a loved one's illness and respond in healthy, formative ways. Also, ask parents and other family members how they are coping with issues related to illness and offer them support in handling changes in the children as well as changes within themselves.

Some congregations keep a kit or box of books, activities, puppets, games and other items on hand to use with children of different ages. These items may be used by trained clergy or lay leaders or they may be loaned or given to parents. This can be an effective way for congregations to demonstrate care.

When the Patient Is a Child

There are unique challenges when the person with a chronic or life-threatening illness is a child. Unlike a temporary illness such as a cold, a chronic illness requires a child to cope with the long-term effects.

Still My Teacher

My precious daughter
Your world turned upside down
And still, you teach me

You have taught me
That you can laugh
Even as the tears flow

You have taught me
That strength
Is not muscle nor bone

You have taught me
That time is not something to measure
But something to live

You have taught me
Not to have hope
Instead to have faith

You have taught me
Winning isn't when you finish
But doing the best
with each step you take

RICHARD FISHER, CHILDREN'S PROJECT ON
PALLIATIVE AND HOSPICE SERVICES

Children often do not understand the cause of illness and may become angry with health care providers or parents when the illness does not go away. Their physical conditions or treatments may cause unwelcome changes to daily activities and bring unwanted attention or teasing. They may blame themselves or others for the situation.

Clear, honest, accurate and age-appropriate information helps children better understand their illness and cope with changes related to it. (See "Supporting Children Living With Illness," below.)

Teenagers with chronic or life-threatening illness often experience the conflicts of adolescence as part of their illness. At a time when the teenager wants to assert independence and sense of self, he or she also must deal with an illness that creates dependence on health care providers and family members. In addition to offering honest and accurate information, family members and health care providers can help by engaging the teenager in decisionmaking processes as fully as possible.

Supporting Children Living With Illness

Here are some tips for anyone who wants to talk with a child about his or her illness.

- Let the child know you will love him or her no matter what he or she says or thinks. Repeat this often.

- Use comforting language and a tone of voice that expresses confidence and warmth.

- If you don't feel completely comfortable talking about goals and hopes, take a few moments to think about how you have talked about other difficult issues with the child and draw upon that experience. Try to use those same ways to engage the child so he or she feels safe.

- Trust your instincts to help you determine how much to say and when. The right moments will appear—and when they do, you can talk with the child lovingly and confidently.

- If your timing is off, just be patient. The child will let you in when he or she is both able to talk and needs to do so.

- Young children naturally focus on more concrete information. Make sure the child understands the plan for today and what's going to happen in the next few hours or the next couple of days.

- Older kids often try to go it alone. They may find it easier to talk to peers with similar medical conditions. Ask the child's medical team about appropriate chat rooms and making contact with other children with similar experiences.

- Reassure the child that you will do whatever you can to prevent pain and help him or her cope with any changes.

- Ask to meet with a child life specialist at the hospital or clinic who can help the child talk about feelings and fears through conversation or play therapy.

ADAPTED FROM CARING CONNECTIONS: WWW.CARINGINFO.ORG.

Additional Resources on Children and Illness

For Parents and Congregational Caregivers

How to Help Children Through a Parent's Serious Illness: Supportive, Practical Advice From a Leading Child Life Specialist, **by Kathleen McCue and Ron Bonn; St. Martin's Griffin, 1996**

Includes information such as what to tell a child about the illness, how to recognize early warning signs in a child's drawings, sleep patterns, schoolwork and eating habits and when and where to get professional help.

Partnership for Parents: www. partnershipforparents.org

Website offering useful information for all stages of illness from initial diagnosis to grief support. Materials are available in English and Spanish.

Talking With Your Child About His or Her Illness

Brochure offering guidance for family and friends supporting a child through serious illness, available at www.caringinfo.org/resources.

When a Parent Has Cancer: A Guide to Caring for Your Children, **by Wendy Schlessel Harpham; Harper Paperbacks, 2004**

Guidance for parents challenged with the task of raising children while struggling themselves with a potentially life–threatening disease. Included is Becky and the Worry Cup, an illustrated children's book that tells the story of a young girl's experiences with her mother's cancer.

When Someone Has a Very Serious Illness: Children Can Learn to Cope With Loss and Change, **by Marge Heegaard; Woodland Press, 1992**

A resource for helping children learn the basic concepts of illness and how to cope at different stages of life.

Additional Resources for Children on Illness

Art with Heart:
www.artwithheart.org

Nonprofit organization that empowers youth facing trauma, illness or other crises through books and resources that support expression of both their suffering and strength.

Here for You: Helping Children Cope With Serious Illness:
www.coordinatedcare.net

This program consists of an original Sesame Street DVD along with tips to help facilitate conversations between children and parents, caregivers or health professionals to encourage children to express their feelings and concerns about their illness.

Little Tree: A Story for Children With Serious Medical Illness, **by Joyce C. Mills; Magination Press, 1992**

Story for children with permanent, life-changing injuries or illness teaches coping techniques such as visualization and relaxation exercises. The book includes a "Note for Parents" section. *Reading level: ages 4 to 8*

Our Mom Has Cancer, **by Adrienne Ackermann and Abigail Ackermann; American Cancer Society, 2002**

Account of the year the authors' mother underwent treatment for breast cancer, illustrated by their own drawings. *Reading level: ages 9 to 12*

Paper Chain, **by Claire Blake, Eliza Blanchard and Kathy Parkinson; Health Press, 1998**

Describes a breast cancer diagnosis and treatment, aiming to inform children trying to cope with the anxiety and upset such news brings. *Reading level: ages 4 to 8*

Promises, **by Elizabeth Winthrop; Clarion Books, 2000**

The story of a girl dealing with her mother's chemotherapy. *Reading level: baby through preschool*

Someone Special Is Very Sick, **by Jim Boulden and Joan Boulden; Boulden Publishing, 1995**

Explores feelings children may experience when confronted with a serious illness in a family member—including how the sick person may look, talk and act differently and need medicines and machines. Included are memory pages and graphics to make get-well cards. *Reading level: ages 4 through 8*

Songs of Love Foundation:
www.songsoflove.org

A nonprofit organization providing free personalized songs for chronically and terminally ill children and young adults. Parents, legal guardians or hospital staff can request compositions.

What About Me?: When Brothers and Sisters Get Sick, **by Allan Peterkin; Magination Press, 1992**

Deals with the feelings a healthy child experiences when a sibling is seriously ill: guilt about having somehow caused the illness, fear that the sibling will die, anger over being left out, anxiety about catching the sickness and longing for life to return to the way it was. *Reading level: ages 4 through 8*

What's Happening to Grandpa?, **by Maria Shriver; Little, Brown & Company and Warner Books, 2004**

With insight derived from the author's father's struggle with Alzheimer's, the story encourages awareness and dialogue among family and friends. *Reading level: ages 4 through 8*

Meeting the Needs of Ill People Through Worship

A Song of Ascents

*I lift up my eyes to the hills—
from where will my help come?
My help comes from the Lord,
who made heaven and earth.*

*He will not let your foot be moved;
he who keeps you will not slumber.
He who keeps Israel
will neither slumber nor sleep.*

PSALM 121: 1-4

Serious illness is most frequently integrated into worship services during prayers for those who are ill, specific intercessory prayers and prayers for the faithful. For many faith traditions, these prayers provide significant ways of creating a circle of care as faith leaders and members pray for one another. But congregations also have the opportunity to consider additional ways of integrating illness and caregiving into worship. In addition, faith communities can make worship services more accessible for people experiencing illness.

As you plan to support those with illness during worship, consider incorporating special services, seasons and worship ideas, as discussed below.

Special Worship Services

To minister directly to the needs of people living with illness and those who care about them, congregations may create special worship services to offer support.

Healing Services

Just as faith traditions differ in their concepts, practices and understandings of healing, they also offer a variety of types of healing services. Depending on the needs of your particular congregation, you may consider scheduling healing services on a regular basis— annually, quarterly, monthly or weekly.

The Practice of Anointing the Sick

Anointing the sick is one of the seven sacraments of the Roman Catholic Church. Also called "unction of the sick," this sacrament is administered by a priest to those who are in extreme physical danger due to sickness or old age. The sacrament is alluded to in Mark 6:13, and the chief Christian text concerning anointing of the sick is James 5:14-15.

According to Catholic teaching, the sacrament gives grace for the state into which people enter through sickness; imparts the Holy Spirit against anxiety, discouragement and temptation—and conveys peace and fortitude.

Various Protestant communities also anoint the sick, though they may differ in their frequency, rituals and beliefs surrounding the practice. Some denominations believe that physical healing will occur as a result of anointing, while others consider healing to be a spiritual event that may not result in physical healing.

Unlike the Roman Catholic Church, most Protestant communities do not associate anointing with impending death; in fact, some Protestant communities offer anointing quite frequently to members who feel the need for any sort of healing.

And congregations in Charismatic and Pentecostal traditions may do anointing with little ceremony or ritual. In these traditions and in many others, "laying on of hands" is often associated with the practice of anointing as the minister or congregation members physically touch the person who is ill as they pray.

(For more on specific denominational resources, see the Duke Institute on Care at the End of Life's website: www.iceol.duke.edu.)

Services for
People With Memory Disorders

Regular worship services can be too lengthy for people with memory disorders. In addition, people with Alzheimer's and other forms of dementia may not respond to your current hymns, songs, scripture translations and other worship elements as strongly as they do to familiar sounds, words and rituals.

For example, one man with Alzheimer's, sitting in a wheelchair with a blank stare, began moving his lips and singing when he heard the familiar hymn "Amazing Grace." A woman with Parkinson's-related dementia joined in saying familiar verses from scripture when they were read aloud in worship. Although she could not remember what had happened earlier that day, she could recite the verses exactly as they appear in the King James translation.

Consider holding worship services specifically designed for these people. Incorporate short prayers, familiar songs and scriptures. Use older versions of hymns and rituals as well as traditional scripture translations. If you choose to include a sermon or meditation, keep it short. Use familiar sources to encourage interaction.

You may choose to open this up to the community. Consider partnering with local skilled care facilities, chaplains and other professionals and organizations working with people with memory disorders to create such services. (See Worship Service Intervention, page 60, for more ideas on services for people with memory disorders.)

Worship for Those With Specific Illnesses

Many national organizations that promote health and support people with illnesses have established particular days, weeks and months to make people aware of specific conditions and diseases. These designated times can serve as opportunities for your congregation to address particular issues and to focus education, worship, support and prayer.

For example, February is American Heart Month, March 25 is American Diabetes Alert Day and November is dedicated as National Alzheimer's Disease Awareness Month. For a full list, including dates, go to the U.S. Department of Health & Human Services' website at www.healthfinder. gov/libraryinfo. This website also includes the contact information for sponsoring organizations, which often link to additional resources.

In addition to nationwide awareness days, weeks and months, a number of faith traditions and denominations have adopted special weeks and days that recognize and provide information about wellness, disabilities and illness. For example, the Association for Brethren Caregivers has developed a Health Promotion Sunday, the Presbyterian Church (USA) has organized a Health Awareness Day and the United Church of Christ has adopted a Health and Welfare Sunday as well as an Access Sunday and Disabilities Week. In addition to designating special weeks and days, these denominations offer resources for congregations to use.

In your congregation, for example, you may hold a "Blessing of the Hands" service honoring nurses. This service can be held during the beginning of May, to coincide with National Nurses Week. Congregations have used this date to honor the service of community nurses, especially including faith community nurses.

Special Seasons and Holidays

Many people with illness feel the most isolated around the holidays because they cannot be involved with the congregation's services and special events. These are times for congregations to be especially sensitive to those who may feel left out.

For example, volunteers in Jewish congregations may observe Shabbat with those who cannot leave their homes or help ill or caregiving members prepare for Passover. Volunteers in Christian congregations may deliver lilies from the Easter worship service and share a reading or hymn with them. Volunteers may visit during Advent and light an Advent candle with members who cannot attend worship. (For a listing of services for specific denominations, see the Duke Institute on Care at the End of Life's website: www.iceol.duke.edu.)

Weekly Worship

Congregations should address issues related to illness regularly, during weekly worship. As members experience elements of worship that incorporate issues of illness and wellness, they can feel the community's support for them. Additionally, they can be reminded of other members who are experiencing these issues and extend the circle of care for those who are in need.

Scripture. As you come upon or choose scripture to be read during worship, do not omit or hurry through readings that address illness, caring or times of distress.

Readings, poems, liturgies and prayers. Incorporate readings into your worship from sources outside of scriptures that address illness, healing and caregiving. Use the quotes and poems included in the toolkit as a starting place. If intercessory prayer is part of your faith tradition, pray specifically

for caregivers in addition to people who are ill.

Anointing. If appropriate with your faith tradition, consider offering opportunities for anointing during a regular worship service.

Attending to children. Use children's books as a starting place for sermons specifically for them that deal with issues of serious illness. (See the additional resources on pages 56 and 57.)

Adding personal stories or testimonies. Offer opportunities during worship for congregational members to share their own experiences of illness. Encourage people to share their struggles and questions, as well as their stories of hope and transformation.

Tailoring sermons and homilies. Draw on scriptures, books, movies, personal experiences, situations in the news and other sources to incorporate issues of illness, healing and caregiving into your sermons and homilies.

Commissioning and blessing. During regular worship services, commission members of support teams who are preparing to serve as volunteer caregivers. For example, congregations that make prayer shawls or quilts could offer special blessings over these and pray for their recipients during worship services. (For more about support teams and prayer shawl and prayer quilt ministries, see pages 49 and 53.)

Recognizing service. Recognize and honor caregivers specifically during worship. In addition to recognizing family caregivers, also acknowledge volunteer caregivers such as friendly visitors, lay ministers and support teams.

Mi Sheberakh: May the One Who Blessed

May the One who blessed our ancestors—
Patriarchs Abraham, Isaac, and Jacob,
Matriarchs Sarah, Rebecca, Rachel, and Leah—
bless and heal the one who is ill:

_____

son/daughter of _____ .

May the Holy Blessed One
overflow with compassion upon him/her,
to restore him/her,
to heal him/her,
to strengthen him/her,
to enliven him/her.

The One will send him/her, speedily,
a complete healing—
healing of the soul and healing of the body—
along with all the ill,
among the people of Israel and all humankind,
soon,
speedily,
without delay,
and let us all say: Amen!

TRADITIONAL JEWISH PRAYER FOR THE SICK

Additional Resources on Worship Planning

Beliefnet: www.beliefnet.com

Website offers a library that includes prayers from different faith traditions for times of illness, death, aging, comfort, healing, hope, strength and courage, loneliness and others.

Commissioning to a Caring Ministry Within a Congregation, **by Steven H. Shussett; National Health Ministries, Presbyterian Church (USA)**

Provides a sample commissioning ceremony for volunteers in caring ministries, free online at www. pcusa.org/nationalhealth/ careteams/commissioningservice. pdf.

Guides for Interfaith, Protestant and Catholic Caregiving Services, **by National Family Caregivers Association (NFCA)**

Three booklets—for an interfaith service, a Protestant service and a Catholic service—containing guides and timelines for caregiving services as well as bulletins for model services. Available free at www.nfcacares. org/national_family_caregiver_ month/guide.cfm.

Healing Liturgies for the Seasons of Life, **by Abigail Rian Evans; Westminster John Knox Press, 2004**

Offers worship and devotional resources, specific healing liturgies for injury, illness, death, separation, retirement and a host of other major life events, from a wide variety of religious traditions.

Healing Services (Just In Time!), **by James K. Wagner; Abingdon Press, 2007**

Included are complete services of Holy Communion, Healing and Wholeness; Praise, Prayer, and Anointing; and Prayer, Confession, and Laying on of Hands. Services are meant for Sunday morning worship; retreat settings; small group experiences hospital, nursing home and home visitations; personal counseling sessions.

Moments of Grace: Hymns, Worship Services & Meditations for Caring and Healing Ministries, **by David Christian, John Eckrich and Arden Mead; Creative Communications for the Parish, 2002**

Pamphlet includes liturgies, hymns on wellness and healing and meditations for people dealing with illness.

Ritualwell: www.ritualwell.org

Website focuses on Jewish ritual innovations for holidays, lifecycles and Jewish customs. Includes rituals and prayers surrounding healing, growing older and death and grief.

Speaking to Silence: New Rites for Christian Worship and Healing, **by Janet S. Peterman; Westminster John Knox Press, 2007**

Includes a broad spectrum of rituals for individuals and families, congregations and the wider community. Describes a process for creating new rituals and suggests ways to adapt existing worship materials to new settings.

Worship Service Intervention, **by the New York Department of Health**

Resource for residential facilities regarding worship services for people with dementia. Addresses goals and benefits, program structure, rituals, troubleshooting and references. Under "Forms," this website includes a "Sample Worship Service" that addresses different faith traditions at www.health. state.ny.us/diseases/conditions/ dementia/edge/interventions/ worship/index.htm.

How This Toolkit Can Help	62
Understanding Death and Dying	62
The Beginning of the End	62
Understanding the Dying Process	63
At Death	66
Following Death	66
Death of a Child	66
Care at the End of Life	67
Hospice Services	67
Hospitals	68
Nursing Facilities	69
Preparing for the End of Life	69
Legal and Financial Planning	69
Health Care Planning	69
Final Arrangements Planning	70
Advance Care Planning	70
How Faith Communities Can Help	75
Congregational Action Planning	75
End of Life Education	76
Educational Sessions	76
An End of Life Series	80
Congregational Care	80
Pastoral Care	81
Special Needs of Dying Children	82
Lay Congregational Care	83
Incorporating End of Life Into Worship	86
Special Worship Series	86
Weekly Worship	87

Our acceptance of our death influences not only the experience of dying but also the experience of living; life and death lie along the same continuum. One cannot—as so many of us try to do— lead life fully and struggle to keep the inevitable at bay.

FROM *BEING WITH DYING: CULTIVATING COMPASSION AND FEARLESSNESS IN THE PRESENCE OF DEATH,* BY JOAN HALIFAX; SHAMBHALA, 2008

To provide feedback on this toolkit, go to **www.iceol.duke.edu.**

For faith communities, death and dying have always played significant roles in shaping beliefs, practices and congregational life. And yet, the end of life remains a challenging season for many people of faith. Many fast-forward through death, falling into the trap of thinking it happens only to other people or focusing only on "a better home a-waiting." Even the most faithful people can be shocked, unnerved or deeply challenged when facing death and dying.

> *Death is not extinguishing the light; it is only putting out the lamp because dawn has come.*
>
> Philosopher Tagore

Dying, however, is ultimately about living. It raises important spiritual issues such as meaning and purpose, guilt and forgiveness, suffering and redemption, healing and hope. It holds up a mirror to life, challenging people to sort out what matters most. By exploring the end of life journey and the spiritual issues that it brings, faith communities have tremendous opportunities to help members deal with the essentials of both death and life.

How This Toolkit Can Help

While congregations agree that caring for people at the end of life is essential, most are unsure how best to meet the needs of dying people. Many wait until the last minute to reach out, missing significant opportunities to educate members along the way about end of life issues. When the end of life comes, congregations often struggle with how to provide effective support.

This chapter will help you help you:

- teach your congregation about end of life as a part of life

- plan ahead for end of life decision-making so members will be better prepared

- support your members so that care by clergy, lay leaders and members is coordinated and effective, and

- integrate end of life awareness into worship so that the spiritual lives of dying congregants will be remembered and honored.

The information and resources in this chapter complement the strategies and ideas for leadership, education, congregational care, worship, communications and faith community space found in the chapter Creating Unbroken Circles of Care. As you use these resources together, you will be equipped to tailor ministries specifically for people at the end of life. Through your efforts, your congregation will become an unbroken circle of care as people live with death and dying.

Understanding Death and Dying

This section explores the nature of death and dying, describing the dynamics and demystifying the process. It discusses the questions and fears that people of all ages face and the growth and healing that people can experience as they are dying. And it explores how everyone can better integrate death as a part of life, learning more about it now and planning ahead for its inevitability. This understanding is a key first step in supporting those who are going through the process.

The Beginning of the End

When does the end of life begin? Some may answer: "When a person is actively dying." Others may say: "When he or she is living with a life-limiting illness." Still others may claim: "End of life begins at the beginning of life." In reality, there is no single answer.

Since more than 90% of people die from an illness, everyone must cope with the changes that the end of life illness brings. Coping is unique. Some people will be ready to shift from curative care to comfort care, also known as palliative care, when the end of life seems likely. Others will want all forms of aggressive curative treatment possible, including experimental treatments. It is important to understand each individual's goals and values to support him or her effectively through decisionmaking.

Ask Tough Questions

Caring Connections, a program dedicated to improving care at the end of life, urges people to ask tough questions when facing life-limiting illness.

People may ask their health care providers questions such as:

- What decisions will my family and I have to make and what kinds of recommendations will you give to help us make these decisions?

- What will you do if I have pain or other uncomfortable symptoms?

- Will you let me know if treatment stops working so that my family and I can make appropriate decisions?

- Will you still be available to me even when I'm sick and close to the end of my life?

And people may have tough questions for spiritual care providers such as:

- Will you understand and support my need for my spiritual self to be nourished and to grow, even as my physical being deteriorates?

- If I have negative feelings such as frustration, sadness, despair, anger at God or life, will you listen empathetically?

- Will you continue to visit even if I get very sick or can no longer respond?

- Will you visit with my family and help them with their spiritual concerns about my illness?

Asking these tough questions prompts professionals to offer real information and support. It is a way to signal that they understand the importance of making hard decisions and dealing with difficult issues as they arise.

ADAPTED FROM "IF YOU OR SOMEONE YOU LOVE IS VERY ILL... ASK TOUGH QUESTIONS," AVAILABLE AT WWW.CARINGINFO.ORG/RESOURCES.

Understanding the Dying Process

The dying process may happen slowly or quickly, depending on the particular disease or cause and how ready the dying person or family members are for death. Still, there are often common predictors. While end of life care professionals such as hospice and palliative care providers can help dying people and their communities understand the dying process, it is important for everyone to know some of the usual signs and symptoms. Understanding these changes can help prepare clergy and lay caregivers to offer more compassionate care and support while a person is dying.

Dying people often experience a number of interrelated changes.

Physical Changes

The dying person's body begins to shut down, a process that ends when all systems stop functioning. Depending on the dying process, this often occurs in an orderly way.

Some of the earlier physical changes often include:

Decreased eating and drinking. As people near the end of life, their bodies need less food and fluid. This can be difficult for family members because feeding someone is often equated with healing and not feeding is associated with starving. However, because people need less and less fuel as they shut down, forcing them to eat may be more harmful than helpful. It is important to offer food when people are able to eat, but not to force it.

Similarly, decreasing fluids is normal as a body shuts down. Giving a person more fluid than needed can cause fluid retention that brings swelling, greater risk of bedsores, increased vomiting and other discomfort. To help, caregivers can moisten a dying person's mouth to provide comfort.

Pain. Pain may increase or decrease as people are dying, often calling for changes in types and doses of medication. While people sometimes fear that medication may cause death, when pain is effectively managed, death will occur because of the disease, not because of the medication.

Sleepiness. A dying person often sleeps for long periods, sometimes becoming difficult to wake up. As dying progresses, sleeping may increase from hours a day to sleeping all the time, a comatose state. Caregivers may wonder if the person can still hear. Because hearing is known to be the sense that remains during the dying process, it is important for everyone to speak to the dying person as they come and go, telling him or her about the care they are providing and saying things what they would like to say to the person.

Weakness. People often experience increasing weakness, bringing an increased need for help with self-care such as toileting and bathing.

Breathing changes. A dying person's breathing may change, becoming shallow and irregular, with times of apnea, or no breathing, for up to 30 seconds or longer. Alternatively, breathing may become shallow and rapid. It is important for observers to understand this type of breathing, often called "Cheyne-stokes" breathing, is normal. They can help by repositioning the person as needed and offering a calming presence.

Congestion. As people become weaker, they are less able to eliminate congestion. Sometimes the increased congestion causes the development of a noise or "rattle" in the person's throat. While this sound may be scary for those who witness it, it is not painful for the dying person. Decongesting medications and turning the person may help.

Conversations That Really Matter

Ira Byock, physician and end of life expert, identifies five key statements that are important at the end of life.

- Please forgive me. Asking for forgiveness takes courage and risk. Dying people may seek forgiveness from others, from God and from themselves. Asking forgiveness demonstrates a willingness to reconcile a relationship.

- I forgive you. Offering forgiveness in relationships also takes courage. Granting forgiveness as well as seeking it can bring healing in relationships.

- Thank you. Gratitude is an important part of the end of life—appreciating people's contributions, what they have done and who they have been. Gratitude focuses people on the positive aspects of life and brings joy.

- I love you. Because love is so essential to human life, taking the opportunity to express love is most important at the end of life.

- Goodbye. "Goodbye" derives from "God be with you," a blessing that reminds us of God's presence in leave-taking. Saying goodbye is not easy, but it affirms that life is coming to an end. When a family members or friend is able to say goodbye at the end of life, it may give the dying person the permission he or she may need to go through the process. Saying goodbye also is healing for the person who lives on.

For more, see *The Four Things That Matter Most: A Book About Living*, by Ira Byock; Free Press, 2004. For a free self-study reader's guide to use individually or with study groups, go to www.thefourthings.org.

Energy surges. Prior to death, it is not uncommon for people to experience a surge of energy, becoming alert, possibly more lucid, talkative or hungry. For example, one man who had not eaten more than a few bites for several days sat up and ate an entire plate full of cookies during such a surge. While surges can confuse others into thinking the person is recovering, often it is really a rare opportunity for interaction and for people to take care of "unfinished business." When it passes, the symptoms of dying return.

Temperature changes. As a person nears death, circulation decreases. The dying person's hands and arms, feet and legs may feel cooler and develop bluish patches. Nail beds may become bluish as well. The person's skin may become darker where it contacts the bed and other surfaces.

Emotional and Relationship Changes

During the dying process, a person may seek to heal unresolved emotional issues, reconcile relationships and begin saying goodbye.

Some of the emotional and relational changes may include:

Anticipatory grief. As people prepare to die, they often go through a grieving process that may include sadness, anger, depression, anxiety and dread. (To learn more about this, see Anticipatory Grief, page 91.)

Fears around dying. While some people fear death as it approaches, more often people express fear about the dying process itself. Some fear that they will be in pain or will not know how to cope with the changes. Some are afraid of going to sleep and not waking up. Some people are afraid of dying alone. Family, friends and care providers can offer comfort by listening to the dying person's fears and offering support and care aimed at soothing them.

Decreased interaction. Dying people have less and less energy. As a result, they may wish to interact with fewer and fewer people. Talking becomes less important and presence or touch becomes more important. Family and friends must strive to understand that this decreased interaction is normal and not meant to be offensive.

Cognitive Changes

Dying people may experience significant cognitive changes that can cause disorientation for them and concern on the part of family and friends.

Cognitive changes may include:

Confusion. Dying people may become unclear about time, places and the people around them—including close family and friends. This confusion may increase as the dying process progresses. While confusion is normal, it is important to take note of it because confusion may point to an underlying problem such as pain, constipation or another symptom. Caregivers can help with confusion by identifying themselves, speaking clearly and directly and being patient.

Symbolic communication. Some dying people communicate through symbolic language or experiences, often called "nearing death awareness." Statements such as: "I'm going to the station," or "My bags are packed" may be dismissed as confusion by those around them. In reality, such statements, which often connect common activities and places from a person's life, help him or her communicate that a transition is occurring. Another facet of nearing death awareness may be reports of conversations with people who have already died or descriptions of "otherworldly" places.

A dying person may communicate through symbolic language or experiences: "I'm going to the station," or "My bags are packed" signaling a transition is occurring.

A Time for All Things: Healing v. Cure

Along with the question "Why is this happening to me?" dying people may ask why God is not healing them. They may experience the admonitions of others who say: "If you pray hard enough, you will be healed."

While faith communities have differing beliefs on this point, it can be helpful do distinguish between healing and cure. Cure refers to physical remedy. Healing refers to finding wholeness. A person may experience healing in relationship with God or others when a cure is not possible.

According to the book of Ecclesiastes: "To everything, there is a season." The question clergy or lay caregivers may raise is: "What is it a time for now? Is it a time for a physical cure or, since a time of death does come for all of us, is it a time for a different kind of healing?" This broad approach to healing will help all people of faith keep healing in perspective.

While not everyone experiences nearing death awareness, it is important for family and friends of those people who do communicate such experiences by listening, treating them as real and talking about what they mean if possible. This can help dying people who feel they have unfinished business.

Spiritual Changes

As people are dying, significant spiritual changes may take place.

Some normal reactions people experience during the dying process include:

Exploration of beliefs. Dying people often evaluate what they believe in the light of their illness and dying experience. Core beliefs often come to the surface as people clarify the aspects of their faith that matter most to them. Some people will return to beliefs or faith communities they have left; some find new beliefs that fit with their new understanding of life.

Statements of guilt and confession. Dying people may acknowledge guilt in relationship with God and others and need to seek forgiveness. Some may desire to make confession and change their relationship with God. While it is important not to pressure vulnerable people in this area, spiritual reconciliation can be an important part of the dying process.

Seeking peace. Peace often comes as people work through "unfinished business" and find a sense of healing and reconciliation. Many people may do this through growth in their relationship with God, though some may choose not to discuss their spiritual beliefs and experiences with others. It is important to respect each person's wishes and offer support in seeking peace.

Questions of meaning and purpose. People often ask questions such as

• Why is this happening to me?

• Why am I dying this way?

• Why is God doing this to me?

• Why can't I go ahead and die?

These questions are usually an attempt to make sense of what is happening. They are a sign that the person is seeking a new understanding of who they are and what is happening.

The Wish to Die Alone

Many people consider the idea of someone dying alone to be unacceptable. As a result, some family members may sit vigil with dying people to ensure this does not happen. In some circumstances, however, a vigil may go on and on, with the dying person not reaching death.

In reality, there are some people who wish to be alone at the time of death. This sometimes becomes clear in retrospect when the people sitting vigil take a short break for a quick stretch or meal. When they return, they may discover the person died in their brief absence.

When a death like this one occurs, people may experience guilt that they were gone "only a minute." They may be concerned they abandoned the person in the time of greatest need. To the contrary, chances are the person was waiting for just such an opportunity.

In such situations, clergy and other supporters can help by anticipating this when the signs are there.

A solution may be to talk with the family sitting vigil about this possibility and work with them to create some alone time for the dying person. The clergy or other caregiver may spend this alone time with family down the hall or in a chapel, prepared that the dying person may have died or continue living when family members return.

As always, these matters require compassion, skill—and good timing.

As Death Approaches

When people are actively dying, the wide range of changes they experience may become more intense. Dying people often need palliative care—a comprehensive approach to treating serious illness that focuses on the patient's physical, psychological, spiritual and existential needs. Its goal is to achieve the best quality of life available by relieving suffering and controlling pain and symptoms, as discussed on the previous pages.

As death approaches, dying people benefit from supportive presence so they are assured they are not alone, and some may have important things to say to others. Goodbyes may occur individually or in groups, often brought together by clergy or chaplains. (See "What Dying People Need Most," page 81, for tips on how to provide support.)

Dying sometimes appears to be delayed when a person continues active dying for an extended time. This may reflect unfinished business, such as waiting for an important person's wedding, birthday or holiday or a desire to reconcile with an estranged family member or close friend. Dying may also be delayed if others are keeping vigil and the person seems to wish to die alone. It is important for people to be supported in completing this unfinished business as needed and to say what they want to say, including goodbye, as part of the dying process.

At Death

The physical signs are the clearest indicator that death has occurred. Breathing, pulse and heartbeat cease. Pupils dilate and become set. Urine and stools release. The person is unresponsive to word and touch.

These final signs do not happen all at once or in any certain order. When all of these signs occur, the person has died.

Following Death

After death, cleaning and dressing the body is a way to show respect. Family members may wish to be involved and their wish should be honored. It is also important for family or friends to have time with the person's body if they choose.

Following death, other family, friends, professional caregivers and selected funeral or memorial personnel need to be contacted. If there are any irregularities or the death was unattended, the circumstances of the death may need to be evaluated by law enforcement.

Following the immediate response to death, the time for appropriate grief support begins.

Death of a Child

More than 85,000 children die in the United States each year. Whether due to problems at birth, sudden accident or illnesses, children's deaths shatter the sense of the natural order of things. Children are expected to grow up and outlive the adults around them. When they die, their deaths often evoke extraordinary pain and difficult questions, especially for parents and others who care for them. The end of a child's life may prompt a loss of hopes and dreams and a crisis of faith.

Children who can understand they are dying may have many questions. Direct, concrete and honest answers help them most. Dying children also benefit from opportunities to talk about their feelings and fears. It is important to address questions about difficult subjects as truthfully as possible and reassure children that their thoughts and wishes are valued.

Seriously ill children may become quite expert in matters related to their treatment and health. When they begin dying, they may be well aware of what is happening and present a mature understanding of their experience.

It is especially important to include children in decisions about their final medical care if their ages and capacities allow it. For example, younger children may be given choices about how care is delivered, but not about what type of care will be provided. More mature children and teenagers may participate more actively in decisionmaking about treatment plans and other end of life options.

A child's end of life illness can put a strain on the parent's marriage and other family relationships. When a child lives with life-threatening illness, one or more parents often develop an extraordinarily close relationship with him or her during the treatment period. Parents may quit work, move to another town to be closer to particular health care facilities or make other major life changes to secure care for the child. And other children in the family may not receive the same attention as the parents respond to the needs of the child who is ill.

In offering care and support, consider everyone involved. Support may begin with a parent, who is often the primary person coordinating the child's care and treatment. Support may be offered to the child as well as siblings and other family members. Each situation will need to be customized to fit the child and family situation. (See Special Needs of Dying Children, page 82, for more on this.)

Care at the End of Life

Many people are not familiar with the choices available as end of life care and how those choices affect their dying experience.

Hospice Services

Hospice is a growing trend in end of life care. Hospice services are for people who have an illness with a life expectancy of six months or less. Hospice patients opt for comfort care rather than curative care, choosing to live out the end of life as naturally and comfortably as possible. Ironically, patients who choose hospice may be choosing to live longer. A recent study by the National Hospice and Palliative Care Organization found that of 4,493 terminally ill patients, those in hospice lived an average of one month longer than similar patients who did not have such care.

The majority of hospice care is provided in private residences, nursing homes and residential facilities, although it is also administered in hospice inpatient facilities and hospitals.

Hospice care is provided through the joint efforts of physicians, nurses, home health aides, social workers, chaplains, counselors and trained volunteers. They all work together to meet the physical, emotional and spiritual needs of the dying patient and families.

The hospice team:

- manages pain and symptoms, including providing medications related to the life-limiting illness, medical supplies and equipment such as hospital beds, wheelchairs and oxygen

- helps with personal care needs such as bathing and grooming

- offers emotional, spiritual and social support

Hospice patients opt for comfort care rather than curative care, choosing to live out the end of life as naturally and comfortably as possible.

- helps with insurance and other benefit issues

- coaches caregivers on how to provide care

- offers short-term inpatient care if pain or symptoms become too difficult to manage at home or the caregiver needs a break

- helps dying people and family members understand what to expect as the disease progresses and through the dying process, and

- provides grief support to surviving loved ones and friends.

Each person and family in hospice care has a plan of care tailored to specific needs. Hospice patients may receive services as long as their prognosis remains six months or less. If a patient's condition improves, he or she may be released

> *If I survive this life
> without dying,
> I'll be surprised.*
>
> Philospher Mulla Nasrudin

from hospice care; however, the services can resume again when the patient's health declines. Patients may also opt out of hospice if they decide to seek curative treatment or wish to discontinue the service.

Available from both for-profit and nonprofit providers, hospice is most often paid for by Medicare or Medicaid. Most private insurance plans also have a hospice benefit. While some dying people may have some out-of-pocket expenses for hospice care, most hospices provide services regardless of the ability to pay.

A hospice referral must be made by a physician. Potential patients can also contact a local hospice to find out what services are available and if they might qualify. Because the level and types of services different hospice services provide can vary significantly, it is wise to interview representatives of several hospices, asking about certifications and services there. Friends and colleagues may also make recommend local hospices.

Learning about hospice services before they are needed is a good way to reduce stress and make decisionmaking easier when hospice care is needed. (To find out more and for a list of hospices near you, go to www.caringinfo.org.)

Hospitals

While 90% of people say they want to die at home, more than half die in the hospital—more than in any other place. Though hospitals provide emergency care, surgery, treatment and other highly technical services, they often focus on finding a cure, not on care for the dying. This is ironic, since most hospital deaths result from a chronic illness that became incurable.

There are many reasons so many people die in hospitals. Many doctors still equate "cure" with "success" and "death" with "failure." As a result, doctors and other health care providers may offer curative options without talking about the prospect of death or helping patients think through other options. Patients with advancing illness and their family members may keep pursuing curative treatment without understanding or wanting to admit that the measures were no longer working. Some may fear death or be determined to try every procedure available, no matter how slim the survival rate.

Some hospitals are now attempting to address these issues. Emerging hospital-based palliative care services focus on pain management,

symptom control and quality of life. In addition to helping patients be more comfortable at all stages of illness, a palliative care team can help identify when patients need hospice or other end of life support. (To learn more about hospital-based palliative care and to see a list of hospital providers, go to www.getpalliativecare.org.)

Hospital chaplaincy, social work and patient support departments often have expertise in helping patients and families discuss end of life issues and make important choices about care. Illness-specific programs may also have specialists. For example, cancer programs may have staff "navigators" who are also knowledgeable about end of life issues and options.

Of Ethics and Life Support

Perhaps the most ethically challenging end of life situations in hospitals involve patients on ventilators and other forms of life support. End of life decisionmaking in these situations often involves designated decisionmakers, physicians and others. Clinical determinations and the individual's wishes are key. Consulting with the hospital ethics committee may be an important step in the process.

Faith traditions and denominations have different beliefs about removing or continuing these forms of treatment. (For denomination-specific resources in this area, see Duke Institute on Care at the End of Life's website at www.iceol.duke.edu.)

Nursing Facilities

More than 20% of deaths take place in skilled nursing facilities, often called nursing homes. Quality of end of life care in this setting varies significantly. While hospice is usually available in these settings, fewer than 30% of nursing home patients have hospice support when they die. Barriers may include philosophical differences on end of life issues among facility administrators and hospice providers, legal regulations and reimbursement mechanisms.

Because each nursing home's policies are different, it is important for patients and their families to consider the facility's philosophy and policies on end of life care, how staff interact with patients and families on end of life issues and the overall safety and quality of the facility. (To find quality ratings for nursing homes from the Centers for Medicare and Medicaid Services, go to www.medicare.gov and search for "nursing home compare.")

The Danger of Remaining Mum

There are many reasons people avoid talking about death and dying and considering options, such as hospice, that can provide effective care:

Personal fears. Many people are afraid to talk about dying because they fear death itself. Some people believe that talking about death or accepting hospice care will somehow cause death to come more quickly.

Family dynamics. Some family members attempt to protect other members from issues of death and dying. In some families, talking about death is not safe or acceptable.

Cultural differences. A person's culture can have an impact on how he or she understands dying. For example, past and current disparities in health care for African Americans, Latinos and others affect how people in these groups experience health care and trust that the health system is doing everything possible to assist them. As a result, people in minority population groups may be wary of end of life services, unsure that every curative option has been offered. (For more on cultural differences and end of life, go to the Duke Institute on Care at the End of Life's website at www.iceol.duke.edu.)

While many people believe that not addressing end of life issues is the more comfortable route, the reality is that not talking about dying has consequences. When those around them avoid talking about end of life, dying people:

- experience greater isolation

- become less able to participate in decisionmaking, and

- have fewer opportunities to fulfill life wishes and to complete unfinished business.

Though help may come in many forms, from practical assistance to personal support, one of the most important ways to support people through their fears and reservations about dying is to listen to their concerns without judgment. Letting them know that they have options and helping them be informed about their health care choices can make a difference.

Preparing for the End of Life

While many people wait until they face a health crisis to address end of life issues, the most effective way to approach dying is to plan for it. The same barriers that keep people from accessing care at the end of life also keep people from planning ahead. However, by learning about end of life options, making choices known and getting their affairs in order, people ensure that their wishes will be known and honored.

The key areas for planning are described here.

Legal and Financial Planning

Estate planning includes preparing a will, trust or other legal arrangements that direct how a person's assets will be distributed at death. Having an estate plan in place helps ensure that the property will pass to the individual's designated beneficiaries.

Health Care Planning

Half of all Americans will reach a point when they are unable to make decisions about their own medical care. Planning ahead for end of life includes: learning about end of life choices, evaluating choices in the light of beliefs and values, talking

What Memorial Societies Can Do

Whether or not money is the overriding issue in deciding on final arrangements, there is a growing consumer preference to keep them simple. For this reason, many people join funeral or memorial societies—nonprofit consumer groups that help them find local mortuaries committed to dealing honestly with survivors and to charging prices that accurately reflect the value of their services.

The cost to join these organizations is low—usually $20 to $40 for a lifetime membership, although some societies charge a small periodic renewal fee. (Many societies also offer "at-need" memberships, allowing survivors to purchase a membership after a death.) Generally, members receive a form upon joining that allows them to specify the goods and services they want and assures that they'll get them for a specified price. While the cost is set when the agreement is entered, payment is not usually made until after the services are provided.

Societies differ in the specific services they offer, but most can provide information on options and any legal controls that apply to final arrangements.

Finally, many societies also serve as watchdogs, making sure that individuals get and pay for only the services that were specified.

To find a funeral or memorial society near you, look in the Yellow Pages or online under "Funeral Information and Advisory Services."

ADAPTED FROM "PLANNING AHEAD FOR FINAL ARRANGEMENTS" BY BARBARA KATE REPA, WWW.CARING.COM

about choices with family members and professionals and completing documents, such as an advance directive. (To learn more about health care planning, see "Advance Care Planning," page 71.)

Final Arrangements Planning

Making decisions in advance about the desire for traditional burial, green or ecologically sensitive burial or cremation helps family members know how best to honor a person's body following death. It is best to discuss these wishes during life and put specific wishes and directions in writing.

Talking in advance about wishes for organ and tissue donation or making an anatomical gift for scientific research is also important. (For more information, see the U.S. Department of Health and Human Services website at www.organdonor.gov.)

Some people also plan the type of burial container, such as a casket or urn, burial or scattering locations and the services or remembrances they would like to have. Because burials can be expensive, planning ahead can reduce unnecessary costs. Doing some comparison-shopping and accessing information from memorial societies can help. (To learn more, see "What Memorial Societies Can Do" at left.)

Faith communities can also take an active role in helping members plan funerals or memorial services in advance. Helping people consider the type of service they would want and any scriptures, reading, hymns or songs they would like incorporated if possible are helpful steps. Some faith communities keep files of funeral or memorial service wishes members have shared with clergy. When clergy leave a congregation, the files stay so that new clergy will have access to these plans.

Advance Care Planning

Many people are familiar with advance directives—legal documents that communicate personal preferences about end of life care. They may provide a way to communicate wishes and avoid confusion if the person who completed them becomes unable to express wishes and make decisions about medical care.

While laws and forms vary from state to state, in general, advance directives may include:

- *Written instructions for medical care.* Called a living will in many states, this document describes the type of medical interventions a person wants withheld or provided if he or she is close to death from a terminal illness or permanently comatose. Some states provide that the documents take effect in case of other medical conditions—and the descriptions and language vary significantly from state to state. However, living wills generally include a person's desire to avoid or receive "life prolonging" or "life sustaining" medical procedures such as mechanical ventilation, artificial nutrition and hydration and cardiopulmonary resuscitation. Some living wills also offer the option of expressing wishes about organ and tissue donation and mental health care that most often take effect in cases of Alzheimer's or dementia.

*Death
in its way
comes just as much
of a surprise
as birth.*

Author Edna O'Brien

- Written authorization for a decisionmaker. Called a durable power of attorney for health care or a health care proxy in many states, this document names a person who will make medical decisions if the individual is unable to do so. Many states allow the person completing the document to name alternates if the primary named is not available.

Some states have separate forms for the instructions and authorizations. Many others now combine the two into one form often called a directive to physicians or advance directive.

The barriers that keep many people from accessing end of life care, such as fear of death, also keep them from completing advance directives. In addition, people often do not complete these legal documents because they do not fully understand end of life decisionmaking and are not familiar with state forms and laws that relate to them.

Many people who have completed advance directive documents, often as part of estate planning or at the request of a family member, still have questions about them. Even those who have completed documents often still have highly technical questions about them and express concerns that their wishes may not be honored.

This concern is well founded. While completing documents is important, it is generally not enough to ensure that a person's health care wishes will be honored. According to the American Bar Association, studies show that advance directive forms do little to influence end of life decisions unless they are accompanied by informed, thoughtful reflection about wishes and values and personal communication with key potential decisionmakers before a crisis. For completed documents to have the maximum power, it is important for everyone to engage in a more comprehensive approach to planning ahead.

Advance Care Planning: Steps in the Process

Advance care planning is a multi-step process. Tips for engaging in each step of the process are offered here.

Step 1: Explore end of life choices.

To complete informed advance directives, it is important for people to understand potential treatments commonly used to prolong life.

For example, mechanical ventilation is a medical device that assists a person who cannot breathe independently. If a there is the medical prognosis that a person may regain the ability to breath alone, the benefits of sustaining the person with this machine are clear. If the prognosis is that the person will not breath independently again, then exploring end of life choices involves considering whether being maintained on a breathing machine in this condition is what the person would want.

In the case of artificial nutrition or hydration, when food and fluids are given intravenously or by a tube, people planning ahead need to understand both the benefits and burdens. The purpose of artificial nutrition and hydration is to provide food and fluid until a person is able to eat independently. When a person is dying or not expected to regain consciousness, this treatment may become burdensome, providing substances the body cannot process. It may also cause discomfort: fluid retention, swelling and skin breakdown.

Many people equate food with healing and may fear that not providing nutrition and hydration at this time is equivalent to "starving a person." In reality, the person may no longer need to fuel the body. Not administering or continuing artificial nutrition and hydration in these situation can be a compassionate choice.

Learning more about these and other treatments such as providing CPR and antibiotics at the end of life helps people make better choices.

Step 2: Reflect on beliefs and values.

Truly effective advance care planning reflects an individual's particular beliefs and values. By evaluating what quality of life means, end of life choices may become more clear. For example, if a person has an illness with no chance of recovery and is no longer able to recognize or interact with family or friends, how strongly would he or she feel about being kept alive through medical intervention? (One way to consider quality of life issues is to complete a worksheet such as the American Bar Association's "Are Some Conditions Worse Than Death?" at www.abanet.org/aging/toolkit/tool2.pdf.)

Addressing spiritual and religious beliefs about end of life is another important part of reflecting. People who explore beliefs and values, particularly the spiritual and religious questions involved, will be more likely to specify end of life choices that fit their beliefs. This important step will help them make choices about their final medical care that will fully honor their living.

Step 3: Discuss choices with others.

While many people find it difficult to talk about end of life choices, it is one of the most important things they can do in advance care planning.

There are a number of other people who may be involved in such conversations:

Health care decisionmakers. It is vital for people to talk with their designated agents in health care power of attorney or proxies about the kind of care they would want at the end of life. Because these agents may be asked to make difficult, time-sensitive decisions in a complex, often confusing medical environment, it is important to select a person who can stay cool under pressure, make thoughtful medical decisions, communicate clearly and concisely and be able to advocate for the care choices expressed. While some people select their closest relative as that decisionmaker, others choose more distant relatives or friends for this role.

Once the person is selected and agrees to serve if needed, it is important to talk about specific end of life choices spelled out in advance directives as well as the more philosophical matter of what quality of life means.

Such discussions may include:

- beliefs and values that inform end of life care

- what quality of life means

- specific preferences about medical interventions such as artificial ventilation, artificial nutrition and hydration and other treatments

- any concerns or fear about end of life care, and

- any hopes at the end of life.

In these conversations, it is important for people to talk about what they want, as well as what they do not want. Having in-depth conversation about these issues better equips the health care decisionmaker to make choices that fully reflect the patient's wishes.

Family members. No matter who is selected, it is important to communicate who the decisionmaker is to other family members, as well as particular wishes for end of life care in general. For example, if a person does not want to be maintained on a ventilator beyond the point of hope for a recovery, sharing this

A GUIDE FOR SPIRITUALITY AND ADVANCE CARE PLANNING

Key spiritual questions individuals can ask that can relate to advance care planning can include:

- What beliefs, teachings and scriptures inform end of life choices?

- What role do prayer or contemplation play preparing in advance care planning?

- What role do a sense of meaning and purpose in life play in making end of life choices?

While some people may point to a specific belief or scripture that addresses end of life concerns, many people of faith reflect on end of life decisionmaking in the larger context of spiritual and religious beliefs.

For example, the Evangelical Lutheran Church in America's opening statement on end of life decisions offers guiding convictions such as "Life is a gift from God. The integrity of the life processes that God has created should be respected. Both living and dying should occur within a caring community. Each person's preferences regarding treatment decisions are to be respected. Hope and meaning in life in times of suffering and adversity is possible." When individuals clarify their own spiritual beliefs about end of life issues, the advance care planning choices become clearer.

Increasingly, denominations and faith traditions offer specific statements, guidance or resources on complex advance care planning issues. For an extensive listing of these resources, see "Across Cultural and Spiritual Traditions" on the Duke Institute on Care at the End of Life website: www.iceol.duke.edu.

TIPS FOR TOUGH CONVERSATIONS:
TALKING ABOUT END OF LIFE WISHES

Starting the conversation about end of life wishes can feel awkward and scary. Some events or situations that might prompt discussion include:

- the health crisis, illness or death of a family member, friend or noted person

- newspaper articles, movies, TV shows, magazines or books

- annual medical check-ups

- legal or financial planning, and

- a sermon on end of life issues.

Knowing how to discuss advance care planning choices with family members and others can be difficult. Here are some ideas to help prepare for these important conversations:

Start with yourself. Begin by discussing your own wishes rather than asking another person about his or her choices.

Choose the time and place. Tell the other person in advance that you have something important you would like to discuss, rather than catching him or her unprepared for a serious conversation.

Don't change your normal communication style. For example, if you are more comfortable communicating on the phone rather than in person, start there.

Anticipate possible reactions and your responses. Use communication strategies you have found successful in the past.

Pay special to attention to those who are most likely to disagree. Talking with them in advance creates the best chance they will not cause conflict when difficult decisions are being made.

Seek out opportunities to communicate with groups. For example, one man set up a conference call with his four sons who lived in different parts of the country so he could tell all of them at the same time what he wanted, laying the groundwork for them to reference this conversation later. Because he found it too difficult to talk about these issues in person, doing it over the phone was easier for him.

The more often one broaches conversations with family members and others about end of life wishes, the more natural they become. Often it takes several conversations. However, this is worth the effort. In addition to increased assurance that wishes will be honored, many people discover that these important life conversations strengthen relationships with people they love.

information with concerned family members would make it easier for the designated agent to carry this wish out later if needed.

Often, a family member who has been distant or in conflict will be the one who objects to making difficult decisions such as removing ventilation. Talking with all family members during the advance care planning process can help reduce such conflicts at the end of life, bringing the focus back to the kind of treatment the individual wants.

Doctors. Talking with a doctor about wishes for final medical care helps people learn more about potential treatment options and helps the doctor better understand the patient's wishes. By raising the topic with primary care doctors during a physical or a consult visit to discuss end of life care, patients can discuss:

- the particulars of possible end of life treatments

- pain management

- personal concerns about quality of life, and

- individual philosophies about end of life.

Meeting with a doctor to discuss advance directives can help clarify decisions and ensure that the doctor understands the patient's wishes. It can also be helpful for the patient to tell the doctor what family members know about his or her wishes and to provide copies of completed advance directives for the medical file. While a primary care physician may not be the one who provides care during hospitalization, his or her understanding and support for end of life wishes can make a big difference when it comes time to carry them out.

Additional Resources for Clergy and Lay Leaders

Being With Dying: Cultivating Compassion and Fearlessness in the Presence of Death, by Joan Halifax; Shambhala, 2008

Emphasizes the ability to open up to and rely on inner strength, helping others who are suffering to do the same. Incorporates stories from the author's experiences as well as guided exercises and contemplations from a Buddhist perspective. For more information, go to www.upaya.org.

Clergy End of Life Education Enhancement Project: A Guide for Clergy to Provide Support to Family at the End of Life

The Hospice Foundation of America offers this online self-study curriculum with modules such as: Cultural Considerations at the End of Life, The Dying Process: Medical Perspectives and Psychological Issues and End of life Options: Advance Care Planning and Service Options. The free curriculum is available at www.hospicefoundation.org.

Clergy to Clergy: Helping You Minister to Those With Illness, Death and Grief, by Kenneth Doka; Hospice Foundation of America, 1993

Audio series designed to provide clergy with a simple way to learn more about issues related to care at the end of life, death, grief and bereavement. Each topic is conversational in format and includes practical suggestions and coping strategies. End of life topics include: The Funeral Ritual— Empowering Healing and When a Child Dies.

Dying Well: The Prospect for Growth at the End of Life, by Ira Byock; Riverhead Books, 1998

Offers a realistic yet compassionate approach to the hard questions asked by dying patients and their families. Focuses on making the end of life meaningful. For more information, go to www.dyingwell.org.

Final Journeys: A Practical Guide for Bringing Care and Comfort at the End of Life, by Maggie Callanan; Bantam, 2009

Guide to understanding the special needs of the dying and those who care for them, offered by a hospice nurse. Illustrates ways to meet the physical, emotional and spiritual challenges of this difficult and precious time and clarifies medical and ethical concerns, explaining what to expect at every stage.

A Good Death: Challenges, Choices and Care Options, by Charles Meyer; Twenty-Third Publications, 1998

Explores practical, real world language about death, offering alternatives to traditional "high-tech" treatment, and the role of spirituality.

Growth House: www.growthhouse.org

Provides online access to reviewed resources for end of life care. Topic areas include major issues in hospice and home care, palliative care, pain management, grief, death with dignity and quality improvement.

Handbook for Mortals: Guidance for People Facing Serious Illness, by Joanne Lynn and Joan Harrold; Oxford University Press, 1999

Guide for individuals facing death that helps them live with serious illness, learn what to expect, find meaning and ways to cope with loss and manage pain and other symptoms. Disease-specific information, end of life decisionmaking and resource lists are included.

Jewish Ritual, Reality and Response at the End of Life: A Guide to Caring for Jewish Patients and Families, by Mark A. Popovsky; Duke Institute on Care at the End of Life, 2007

Guide to Jewish beliefs and practices around illness, death and loss. Practical suggestions for responding to complicated situations where clinical, religious and cultural issues are entwined.

The Needs of the Dying: A Guide for Bringing Hope, Comfort and Love to Life's Final Chapter, by David Kessler; Harper, 2007

Identifies key needs: to be treated as a living human being, have hope, express emotions, participate in care, get honesty and spirituality and be free of physical pain. Helps family members and dying patients communicate with doctors, with hospital staff, children and one another.

Partnership With the Dying: Where Medicine and Ministry Should Meet, by David H. Smith; Rowman & Littlefield Publishers, 2005

Details how congregations should not only support primary caregivers dealing with end of life issues but could enlist their help in informing congregations about the realities of death.

Practical Ministry Skills: Ministry to the Dying

Produced by Christianity Today International, this self-study course helps establish principles for ministry during final days and hours. Curriculum include: How to Shepherd in the Shadow of Death, Deathbed Questions and After the Death. May be purchased and downloaded at www.buildingchurchleaders.com.

Faith community leaders. Many people benefit from talking with informed clergy or lay leaders about matters of faith and care at the end of life.

Faith community leaders should be prepared to discuss:

- religious or spiritual beliefs about death and dying

- how beliefs and values affect end of life wishes and decisionmaking

- views on pain and suffering, particularly spiritual suffering

- how the person's daily spiritual beliefs and practices fit with particular end of life decisions

- religious or spiritual practices or rituals that can be available in the hospital, home or nursing facility, and

- plans for care at the time of death and for services or celebrations following death, such as memorials or funerals.

By making these conversations part of congregational life, faith communities can help members integrate their end of life wishes and planning with spiritual beliefs and values.

Step 4: Document the choices.

Completing advance directive documents is an integral part of the planning process. Because state laws and forms vary from state to state, including different requirements for witnessing and notarizing, it is important to complete forms in compliance with local laws.

Among the places to obtain them:

- Forms with instructions for all states can be downloaded from Caring Connections at www.caringinfo.org.

- Advance directive documents can be obtained from a patient representative at a hospital.

Once advance directives are completed, individuals keep the original document and provide copies to any proxy and alternate named, family members, doctors and others involved in care. Advance directives should be easily accessible, not locked away in a safety deposit box, in case they are needed quickly.

Step 5: Reassess choices over time.

Documents should be reviewed regularly—experts recommend once a year—to be certain they still accurately reflect values and wishes. It is also good to have additional advance care planning conversations periodically to revisit choices and update other people on any changes.

How Faith Communities Can Help

By informing members about advance directives, offering education and congregational care to help members with all aspects of end of life planning—particularly the spiritual and religious aspects—and by helping members plan for memorials and funeral services, faith communities can have a powerful impact on the end of life experience. As they deal with issues of death and dying, faith communities can bring new meaning and purpose to members' lives. By looking ahead to death, members become better equipped to embrace life in the here and now.

Congregational Action Planning

The chapter Creating Unbroken Circles of Care, starting on page 9, will help you explore creative approaches to leadership development, education, congregational care, worship, communications and supportive and accessible space. This chapter offers models for ministry and resources to use in creating unbroken circles of care specifically around end of life.

Currently, care for persons as they die is delegated to medical professionals and institutions: doctors, nurses, social workers, chaplains, therapists, hospitals, nursing homes and hospices. Each has a critical role to play, but ultimately, as members of our communities, we all must retain the responsibility to see that the needs of dying persons are met.

From *Dying Well*, by Ira Byock; Riverhead Books, 1997

End of Life Education

As your faith community provides education around end of life issues, its members will become more familiar with the key issues people face and the resources available. They will better understand your faith tradition's beliefs related to death and dying. And they will be better equipped to support others during this time and to make their own end of life decisions.

The ideas and resources in this section offer a starting place for planning. Topic ideas for educational sessions on end of life include:

- Exploring End of Life Beliefs
- Finding Meaning and Purpose at the End of Life
- Talking With Children About Death and Dying
- What Happens When We Die?
- Preparing for End of Life Decisions, and
- Talking With Others About End of Life Plans.

Designing educational sessions that incorporate interactive adult learning is most helpful as noted earlier. (See the resources listed on page 79, for more.) You may work with professionals such as hospice care providers, hospital chaplains, eldercare advisors, estate planning lawyers, financial planners and others to help develop sessions for your congregation.

Educational Sessions

Whether you offer end of life education sessions during a designated adult education time such as Sunday School, or create a time such as a weekday evening program, the following model sessions may serve as a helpful guides. They may be used as written or adapted. In addition, as you plan additional sessions, they offer a format you can adapt to other related topics.

---

1   Educational Session 1: Visiting Others Who Are at the End of Life

Many people are unsure what to say to those who are at the end of life. While people who are dying often have less energy and interest in visiting with others, friends and family should not shy away from spending time with them. Often brief, meaningful visits that respect the dying person's situation can have a significant impact for both the dying person and the visitor.

This session helps congregation members better understand what dying people are experiencing so that they can visit effectively.

Opening: 5 minutes

Begin with a scripture, poem or prayer. You may choose of one of the devotional resources in this toolkit or choose your own.

End of Life Experiences: 15 minutes

Ask participants to work together in pairs or small groups to discuss their personal experiences when visiting with friends or family members at the end of life. The experience may be a recent one or from many years ago.

Ask them to discuss the following questions:

- Who do you remember visiting and what was that person's relationship to you?
- Where were you? Were there any sights, sounds and smells that stay with you?
- What was the visit like?
- Are your memories positive or painful ones?
- Was there anything that would have made the visit easier for you?

Encourage participants to share both positive and negative experiences related to the visit. If you have time, invited a few participants to share insights from their small group interactions.

Having a Caring Presence With the Dying: 15 minutes

Use the information in this toolkit to help people understand what dying people experience. (See "Understanding the Dying Process," pages 63 to 66, for more specific information.)

In preparing participants to make visits, discuss the following tips on providing a caring presence. You may choose to copy these tips and distribute them to participants. As you present these tips, ask participants about their experiences with key points as time allows. For example, when discussing preparing for a visit, you may ask if anyone had been nervous before a visit and if they have used these ideas in their own practice. Encourage them to offer additional ideas that have worked for them.

HAVING A CARING PRESENCE WITH THE DYING

WHEN PREPARING FOR A VISIT:

- Pray for the patient, family and self.
- Have no agenda other than being compassionate.
- Take several deep breaths.
- Relax, even though it is normal to feel anxious or afraid.

DURING THE VISIT:

- Plan your visit around the person or facility's visiting times.
- Do not wear perfume or aftershave; people may be sensitive to it.
- Identify yourself clearly.
- Speak softly yet audibly.
- Acknowledge the presence of others in the room.
- Include the patient in your conversation with others.
- Give the patient the opportunity to talk.
- Sit close to the patient, but do not sit on the bed without invitation.
- Remember that person will have limited energy; respect their time.
- Listen with an open heart and mind.
- Medication may affect the person's alertness and schedule. Interact accordingly. Even if the person is nonresponsive, remember that he or she may very well be hearing everything that is said.
- Touch may communicate more than words. Make sure, however, that touch is welcome.

WHEN ADDRESSING SPIRITUAL CONCERNS:

- Be respectful of beliefs different from your own.
- Ask nonthreatening, spirituality-focused questions.
- Offer to pray with the patient if appropriate.

HELP FOR FAMILY AND FRIENDS:

- Be sensitive to spiritual, emotional, physical and social needs and concerns.
- Help with practical matter while you are there if possible. Offer to do an errand on the way or to help with folding laundry or doing dishes.
- Stay with the family for support in crisis or bereavement situations.

ADAPTED FROM THE LIFE PROJECT: WWW.LIFEPROJECT.ORG

Group Discussion: 20 minutes

Either working in one large group or returning to the small groups, ask participants to discuss the following questions about visiting people at the end of life:

- What do you consider most important in visiting people facing the end of life?
- What surprises you most about the tips for making a visit?
- Are there any matters that cause you fear or concern about making a visit?
- What would help you as you make visits?
- Are there more ways your congregation can support people at the end of life or support you as you visit others?

Use any wisdom from these discussions to help plan future education or to improve congregational care.

Closing: 5 minutes

You may close with a prayer, reading, song or brief closing insights from participants on how they feel about making a visit at the end of life.

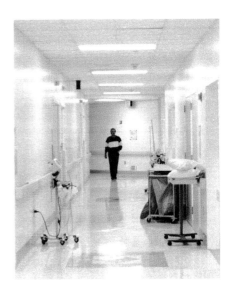

2 Educational Session 2: Planning a Funeral or Memorial Service

Few congregations offer members the opportunity to reflect on the type of funeral or memorial service they would like and what they would like included. Since planning these events is such an integral part of faith community life, offering an education session on the topic can be a meaningful step in providing this ministry.

This session helps congregation members discuss their wishes for funeral or memorial services and to communicate those wishes to family, friends and clergy.

Opening: 5 minutes

Begin with a scripture, poem or prayer. You may choose of one of the devotional resources included in this toolkit or choose your own.

Reflecting on Funerals and Memorial Services: 15 minutes

Ask participants to work together in pairs or small groups to recall and reflect upon funerals and memorial services that stand out for them.

Ask them to discuss the following prompts:

- Describe a funeral or memorial service that was most meaningful for you. Whose service was it? What was the setting? What was most significant or memorable for you in that service?

- When you think about the services you have attended, what did you like the most? What did you like the least?

- Have your views on funerals or memorial services changed over the years?

Learning About the Congregation's Practices: 10 minutes

Faith communities have different liturgies and policies around services. Some faith communities have clearly established guidelines regarding content of the services, music, the roles of clergy and laypeople, honoraria and other matters. If your congregation has funeral planning guidelines, distribute them and review with participants. Ask for questions or feedback. If your congregation does not have written guidelines, discuss your faith community's traditions, common practices and options for funerals or memorials.

You may also use this opportunity to share funeral resources, including faith community information about burial, cremation and green burial as well as information or resources from funeral or memorial societies. (See "What Memorial Societies Can Do," page 70, for more on this.)

Planning a Funeral or Memorial Service: 15 minutes

People often reflect that the most meaningful services are often the most personal ones. In planning for services, offer people as many options as possible. No matter how formal your congregation's customary practices, be sure to identify the points where people have choices.

Ask people to work individually to identify:

- the location and type of service

- who they would like to preside

- scriptures, quotes or other readings

- prayers or other sacred meditations

- hymns or other music

- any special ritual for remembering, and

- other specific instructions or wishes.

You may use this list to develop a worksheet that fits with your congregation or use a funeral planning sheet already in use. (An additional funeral or memorial service planning guide, "Leaving a Legacy," is available from Caring Connections at www.caringinfo.org in the Marketplace. It can be ordered in bulk for congregational use.)

Sharing Plans With Others: 10 minutes

Ask participants to return to their pairs or small groups to briefly discuss wishes for their own funeral or memorial plans. Invite them to discuss any questions they still have remaining about the planning.

Closing: 5 minutes

Encourage participants to continue working on their plans after the class. Invite them to share their plans with family members and with clergy. If the congregation maintains files for funeral plans, offer them that option. Close with a brief scripture or reading drawn from your traditional funeral or memorial service. Send them out in peace.

These two teaching sessions (pages 76-78) are excerpted from Engaging With Compassion: Educational Sessions for Congregations Around Illness, End of Life and Grief, *by James L. Brooks, available from Project Compassion: www. project-compassion.org.*

Additional Resources on Advance Care Planning

Consumer's Tool Kit for Health Care Advance Planning

Contains a variety of self-help worksheets, suggestions and resources. Helps readers with discovering, clarifying and communicating what is personally important in the face of serious illness. Available online from the American Bar Association: www. abanet.org/aging/toolkit/home.html.

Five Wishes

Helps readers express desired treatment if they are seriously ill and unable to speak for themselves, including medical, personal, emotional and spiritual needs. Also encourages discussing your wishes with your family and physician. Available in 20 languages. Individual copies may be ordered, or the document may be ordered in bulk for congregations and large groups. Contact Aging with Dignity: www.agingwithdignity.org/ 5wishes.html or call 888-594-7437.

Getting It Together/Passing on Thoughtfully

Workbook designed to help gather, organize and communicate important information about legal, financial and health affairs, final arrangements and significant life events. Available in printed or CD format individually or in bulk. Contact Project Compassion online at www.project-compassion. org or call 919-402-1844.

Isn't It Time We Talk?

Workbook designed to help individuals and families plan for the care they want at the end of life includes treatment options, thought-provoking questions about values and goals, tips for discussing the choices made and an explanation of advance directives. Contact the Carolinas Center for Hospice & End of Life Care at www. carolinasendoflifecare.org or call 919-677-4126.

Long Goodbye: The Deaths of Nancy Cruzan, by William H. Colby; Hay House, 2003

Describes the troubling ethical questions of brain death, artificial nutrition and hydration, and medical interventions that can prolong physical existence. A free guide with discussion questions for study groups is available at www. growthhouse.org/books/colby.htm.

Your Life, Your Choices: Planning for Future Medical Decisions

Workbook includes thought-provoking exercises on beliefs and values as well as choices about death and dying. Included are sections about how to talk about individual wishes, tips for starting the discussion and how to prepare a personalized living will. From The Rhode Island Health Literacy Project at www.rihlp.org

Additional Resources on Faith Community Curricula

The End of Life: Exploring Death in America

This National Public Radio series has a website that offers links to evocative photographs and transcripts of radio segments, resources, selections from relevant literature, religious rituals and clinical research. For more, go to www.npr.org/programs/death.

How Then, Shall We Live?: Four Simple Questions That Reveal the Beauty and Meaning of Our Lives, by Wayne Muller; Bantam, 1997

Focuses on four questions: Who am I? What do I love? How shall I live, knowing I will die? What is my gift to the family of the earth? Stories are interwoven with meditations, daily practices, poems and teachings from the great spiritual traditions.

On Our Own Terms: Moyers on Dying

Four-part, six-hour Public Broadcasting Station series available on DVD addresses numerous issues related to care at the end of life. Includes a website with a free program guide, questions for discussion and additional resources in English and Spanish is available at www.pbs.org/wnet/onourownterms.

Partners in Caring: Strengthening Clergy and Clinician Collaboration at the End of Life—A Case Study, Duke Institute on Care at the End of Life, 2008

This case study explores the perspectives of a patient with a terminal diagnosis, his family, pastor and doctor. Easily adaptable for a congregational forum or educational session. Available from the Duke Institute on Care at the End of Life: www.iceol.duke.edu.

Tuesdays With Morrie: An Old Man, a Young Man and Life's Greatest Lesson, by Mitch Albom; Doubleday, 1995

Account of the author's reconnection with his old professor who was living with Lou Gehrig's disease and facing death while sharing memories, regrets, fears and philosophical insights. A reading group guide with discussion questions is free online at www. randomhouse.com/features/ morrie/guide.html.

Will the Circle Be Unbroken?: Reflections on Death, Rebirth and Hunger for a Faith, by Studs Terkel; Ballantine Books, 2002

Stories and reflections on death. People famous and unknown offer wise words, meaningful memories and compassionate predictions about the experience of life's end and what may come after.

An End of Life Series

Because the issues around death and dying are so diverse and complex, a multi-part series covering these topics may be the best fit. This gives you the opportunity to explore topics more fully and to build community with participants.

If developing your own multi-part series seems too ambitious, consider accessing ready-to-use curricula designed for faith communities. Some are available free online. While these resources may need some adaptation to fit your congregation, they offer an excellent starting place. To make offering such a series even easier, it may help to partner with end of life professionals in your congregation or community who will facilitate or co-facilitate. As you plan, be sure to include the spiritual, emotional and social implications of end of life as well as participants' experiences.

Congregational Care

Offering Presence

Sit and breathe with your loved one, matching your rhythms.

Sit and meditate with your loved one, matching your visions.

Sit and pray with your loved one, matching your deepest longings.

FROM *GRACEFUL PASSAGES: A COMPANION FOR CARING AND DYING*, BY MICHAEL STILLWATER AND GARY MALKIN; COMPASSION ARTS, 2000

The models, tools, tips and stories about congregational care at the end of life offered here complement the more general congregational care materials and resources in the earlier chapter, Creating Unbroken Circles of Care. Before you begin, be sure to engage in the recommended self-reflection exercise and congregational assessment in that chapter and review the general approach to congregational care. As you prepare yourself and your congregation to become an unbroken circle of care around end of life, consider the range of resources included here.

Additional Resources for Educational Series

Compassion Sabbath Resource Kit

An interfaith initiative providing clergy and religious educators with tools for addressing the spiritual needs of dying people and their families. The Compassion Sabbath resource kit offers six prepared sessions and guides about end of life and a five-session Caring Conversations program. Contact the Center for Practical Bioethics for information on purchasing the resource kit at: www.practicalbioethics.org.

The Complete Life

Developed by Kokua Mau, the end of life care coalition in Hawaii, this interactive curriculum, originally designed for faith communities, includes 17 one-hour sessions. Some sessions related to end of life include: Cultural Beliefs in Death and Dying, Saying Good-Bye and Putting Affairs in Order. The coursebook and PowerPoint slides are available free at www.kokuamau.org.

Generation Why Bible Studies—Deal With It: The Bible on Death and Dying

An educational series for youth that includes five sessions discussing the reality of death, questions of despair, depression and suicide. For more information, go to www.mph.org/flr/youth-genwhy.html.

Interfaith Dialogues for End of Life Ministry

Manual for building faith-based ministries to address death and dying through educational session including How We Die, The Details of Dying and Talking about Death With Your Child. The free manual provides instructions for facilitators, outlines for 1½ to 2 hour facilitated sessions and resources for developing faith community engagement. Available at www.mainehospicecouncil.org.

Living Fully, Dying Well, by Rueben Job; Abingdon Press, 2006

Christian resource designed to assist in making careful, wise and prayerful preparation for meeting life's most important moments. This study course for groups of all ages engages participants to talk openly about faith and mortality on topics such as: What Happens When We Die? And Dying Well. The program kit includes a leader's guide with session plans, worship liturgy and video notes. It also includes a participant book, scripture highlights and lists of additional resources, a DVD with video segments for each of the eight sessions, three additional downloadable study sessions for youth and adults and three booklets for congregation members.

Talking It Over: A Guide for Group Discussions on End of Life Decisions

Designed for lay discussion leaders, this guide provides the format and exercises for three one-hour sessions: Exploring Your Personal Views, Talking With Loved Ones and Making Tough Decisions. Available free in English, Spanish and Tagalog at www.sachealthdecisions.org.

Where can I go from your spirit?
Or where can I flee from your presence?
If I ascend to heaven, you are there;
If I make my bed in Sheol, you are there.
If I take the wings of the morning
and settle at the farthest limits of the sea,
even there your hand shall lead me,
and your right hand shall hold me fast.
If I say, 'Surely the darkness shall cover me,
and the light around me become night',
even the darkness is not dark to you;
the night is as bright as the day,
for darkness is as light to you.

PSALM 139:7-12, NRSV

Pastoral Care

When a person makes the transition from illness to the end of life, congregational care takes on a new and different tone. While general pastoral cares skills for supporting people with illness still apply, it is important to understand that at the end of life, people often have decreased energy, reducing verbal interaction. People may communicate less with words and more with gestures or motions.

While silent presence is always important in pastoral care, it becomes particularly significant for many at the end of life. Ministry may include touching or holding a person's hand instead of talking.

At times, pastoral visits and support may focus more on family and friends than the person who is dying. Clergy may talk with these people about the changes that are occurring, what they are experiencing and the spiritual and theological issues that arise.

When people are actively dying, they benefit from supportive presence to assure them they are not alone. Clergy can listen and reflect what people are experiencing and help facilitate important conversations to express forgiveness, gratitude, expressions of love and of goodbye.

WHAT DYING PEOPLE NEED MOST

Perhaps the best way to learn about care for the dying is to listen to what those experiencing it say about what they want. Here are tips gleaned from experiences with dying people compiled by hospice professionals.

DYING PEOPLE MOST OFTEN NEED:

Assurance that they will be cared for, not abandoned.

Assistance in developing final plans and documents.

Communication with family, friends and caregivers that is honest and open, focusing on listening and being heard.

Excellence in delivery of physical care, comfort, privacy, intimacy, sleep, and rest.

Information that is accurate, timely, and reliable.

Management of pain and other symptoms that is responsive to changing conditions.

Permission to express feelings, both positive and negative, including the opportunity to say statements like "thank you, I love you, I forgive you, goodbye."

Opportunities to:

- discuss impending death with selected family and caregivers

- explore the spiritual dimensions of life and death, and

- discuss funeral arrangements

Time to:

- reflect on the implications of the diagnosis and prognosis

- identify and attend to thoughts, feelings and needs

- tell their stories

- reaffirm their identities and the value of their lives

- reflect on and to grieve prior losses and current losses

- attend to unfinished business, and

- be with selected family and friends.

SOURCE: CLERGY END OF LIFE EDUCATION PROJECT; FOR MORE INFORMATION, GO TO WWW. HOSPICEFOUNDATION.ORG.

Clergy may also offer prayer, scripture and rituals individually with dying people and with gathered family and friends. Many traditions have printed resources to use at the time of death. Bearing in mind the deeply personal aspect of death, customize these resources to fit the person and situation as much as your tradition allows.

Gathered circles can be time for sharing together in words of comfort, scripture, prayers, singing, hand holding, rituals such as anointing or lighting a candle—all as appropriate. Remember to keep gatherings brief. Offer what the dying person may want—for example, singing hymns only if the person enjoyed hymns. Always fully include the dying person, forming a circle that includes the person and that is sensitive to his or her level of interaction and energy.

Above all, clergy responsiveness and presence matters most for people who are dying and their families. It reassures them of God's care and of the support of the faith community. For congregations that have mobilized over time to be intentional circles of care, dying becomes less about establishing or re-establishing a relationship with the faith community and more about coming together in support at the time of death.

> *In the depth of the anxiety of having to die is the anxiety of being eternally forgotten.*
>
> Philospher Paul Tillich

Special Needs of Dying Children

How children handle dying is influenced by age, personality, family support, experiences with illness and treatment and other key factors. No matter the child's age or situation, however, it is important that he or she feels loved and supported.

Often parents are the link that dying children have with health providers and others who want to offer support. In supporting the parents, you help them and the child. (For tips on how parents can talk with children about dying, see "Talking With Your Child About His or Her Illness" at www.partnershipfor parents.org. This information can also help clergy and lay leaders who have the opportunity to talk with the child.)

It is also important to be aware of important spiritual questions children may ask, such as:

- Why is God doing this?
- Where am I going when I die?
- Am I going to be happy after I die?

Reassure parents that an answer is not needed. It is acceptable to show uncertainty and for parent and child to comfort one another. If parents do provide an answer, encourage them to offer responses consistent with the family's beliefs. This approach will be reassuring for the child. It can be helpful for chaplains and faith community leaders to talk with children, though it is important for the parents to talk with them first.

Additional Resources for Families With Dying Children

Endings, by Larry Burd; University of North Dakota School of Medicine, 2001

This booklet raises the questions parents need to think about if their child has a terminal illness. Helps generate questions parents need to ask medical staff while making decisions and preparing their child's death.

Goodbye My Child, by Sarah Rich Wheeler and Margaret M. Pike; The Centering Corporation, 1992

Deals with the deaths of children of all ages and includes information on organ donation, autopsies and funeral arrangements. Also deals with the grief experienced by grandparents, siblings and friends.

Partnership for Parents: www.partnershipforparents.org

Created with assistance from parents, doctors, social workers and chaplains, this website offers helpful information for parents at all stages of a child's illness, particularly at the end of life. Materials available in English and Spanish.

Shelter From the Storm: Caring for a Child With a Life-Threatening Condition, by Joanne M. Hilden and Daniel R. Tobin with Karen Lindsey; De Capo Press, 2002

Advice to families of children who are terminally ill. A compassionate roadmap to what the family members may face, what they may be asked to decide and how they might involve their child in the decisionmaking.

Lay Congregational Care

Caregiving models for lay people supporting others living with illness remain effective as people transition into end of life. Programs such as Bikur Cholim, Called to Care, Stephen Ministry and Support Teams (described in detail on pages 48, 49 and 51) can continue to offer care and support if leaders and volunteers are prepared to shift gears and respond to the needs dying people face as described in this chapter. For example, volunteers who are providing support for people who are dying may need to learn more about how to visit. (See "Having a Caring Presence With the Dying," page 77.)

Specialized Support Programs

A number of programs focus solely on care for the dying.

Doulas for the Dying. Just as midwives and doulas offer emotional, spiritual and skilled support during the birthing process, doulas for the dying offer similar support for people going through the dying process. Programs across the country train doulas for the dying. (See http://doulaforthedying.com and www.shiraruskay.org.)

Hospice volunteer partnerships. Some hospices and end of life care coalitions have outreach programs to increase awareness and to equip congregation members to provide support. One example is the Caring Touch Ministry offered by Nathan Adelson Hospice in Las Vegas, Nevada. Volunteers there learn about end of life issues and hospice services and become ambassadors for improving end of life care in their congregations.

Some hospice providers may offer their patient-family volunteer training for your members onsite. While this training will be valuable for individuals interested in caring directly for people who are dying, the hospice may expect participants to become direct service volunteers, so be sure to communicate clearly about expectations and requirements. (To find a nearby hospice or end of life care coalition, go to www.caringinfo.org.)

The Watchman Program. Trained Watchman volunteers serve as liaisons between a faith community and a hospice, sharing knowledge and information about hospice and end of life issues in their congregations. These representatives act as hospice partners, informing church members about services including hospice care and grief support. They may also link congregations with hospice educational programs and communicate congregational needs to a local hospice. The Watchman Program is usually initiated by hospices. (To see if this program or a similar one has been adopted in your area, check with local hospice agencies.)

Creative ministries. In addition to creating prayer quilts and shawls discussed in the chapter Support During Illness, congregations may use music when appropriate as members transition through end of life.

One example is a Threshold Choir, a movement that is growing across the country. These specially trained choirs sing at the bedsides of people who are dying from illness, people in comas, newborns in hospital intensive care units and those who are recovering from illnesses or injuries. Choir members sing in pairs or small groups in hospices, hospitals, nursing homes and private homes when invited by family or caregivers. Threshold Choirs often invite families and caregivers to join in with singing or to participate by listening. They choose songs to respond to personal and spiritual preferences. (See www.thresholdchoir.org.)

Teaming Up: Before and After Death

A 68 year-old man was struggling with advanced lung cancer. His wife, a recent stroke survivor, was overwhelmed trying to provide care. Their faith community created a support team with 10 members who worked together to provide practical, emotional and spiritual support. Coordinating their efforts, team members brought meals, drove the couple to medical appointments and worship services, took them on outings, organized bills, visited frequently and checked in daily. They even made sure that dog walking was covered every day so the couple would not have to give up their pet.

As it became clear the man was dying, the team members talked with the couple about hospice care. They referred him to a local hospice and even met with the hospice chaplain and social worker to ensure continuity of care. During the man's final months, the team continued its support, complementing the services that hospice provided. Among other things, they helped him get his affairs in order. When he died, the team helped plan the funeral.

Following the man's death, team members continued to support the widow. They sponsored a fundraiser for her, helped her find a more suitable place to live and even helped her move. They also made sure she could keep her dog.

Through their faith community, this couple experienced an unbroken circle of care though end of life and into grief. (For more about the team approach, go to www.project-compassion.org.)

Additional Resources for Congregational Care

***Graceful Passages: A Companion for Living and Dying,* by Gary Malkin and Michael Stillwater; Compassion Arts, 2000**

Spoken word and music recording and book designed to help open the conversation around dying, particularly for those facing it directly. A workbook for professionals, Grace in Practice: Clinical Applications for Graceful Passages, is designed for clinicians and caregivers to integrate Graceful Passages into hospitals, hospices, nursing facilities, counseling practices and homecare settings. For more, go to www.gracefulpassages.com.

***Parting: A Handbook for Spiritual Care Near the End of Life,* by Jennifer Sutton Holder and Jann Aldredge-Clanton; The University of North Carolina Press, 2004**

Offers insight from different cultures and faith traditions on spiritual end of life care, serving as a "travel guide" for meaningful companionship— helping someone toward a peaceful transition from this life. Offers ways to move from ordinary conversation to spiritual reflection and to provide comfort for the body, mind and soul.

***Sacred Passage: How to Provide Fearless, Compassionate Care for the Dying,* by Margaret Coberly; Shambala, 2003**

Discusses the "eight stages of dissolution leading to death," a roadmap of the dying process that describes physical, psychological and spiritual changes interpreted through Buddhist tradition. Includes a lengthy, annotated list of recommended readings.

Dealing With Children and Teens

Congregational caregivers need to be aware that young people need special support when someone they love is dying. Because significant attention is often devoted to the people who are dying and their caregivers, children may not receive the attention and support they might normally receive.

Infants and toddlers. The youngest children will not understand death, but they will sense changes and emotions in others around them. They may become irritable and more prone to crying. Infants may change nursing patters and toddlers may experience changes in bowel and bladder functions.

How to help: Keep daily routines as normal as possible. If a child is accustomed to being rocked or fed at a certain time of day, congregation members could take turns keeping the routines going. Offer verbal and physical comfort and affection such as holding, touching and reassuring. Congregational caregivers can offer to hold the child or talk with the child as part of their visit, reinforcing the importance of stopping to spend special time with children.

Younger children. Children may struggle to understand that death is final and irreversible. If they are accustomed to the sick person sleeping and waking up, they may believe death is like sleeping, that the person will wake up again. Some children engage in "magical thinking," believing that they are responsible for a person's death because of something they have done or said. As with infants and toddlers,

young children are affected by the emotions of those around them and may respond with regressive behaviors such as thumbsucking, wetting the bed or clinging to as security blanket. Some may ask questions repeatedly and others may act out feelings because of difficulty verbalizing. Most children only show sadness, anxiety and other emotions briefly, alternating with play.

How to help: Young children benefit from normal routines. Talk with parents about ways you can help keep routines going. Because children express themselves through play, creating opportunities for them to have creative activities such as drawing or working with clay can be helpful. Support parents in answering questions clearly, concretely and honestly, avoiding euphemisms and being direct when there is no answer. Ask children about what they are thinking and feeling, counteracting magical thinking and giving them a chance to be heard.

Older children. Older children begin to understand the finality of death and may be afraid that it is contagious, fearing the death of other loved ones. Some may picture death as a spirit or ghost and have specific questions about the dying process and what happens after death. Problems in school and regressive behavior such as aggression may develop. Some children become fascinated with death and with killing.

How to help: Talking with older children and encouraging open expression of thoughts and feelings, is important. Encourage parents to normalize fears and feelings and respond as fully as possible to questions. Address any distortions or misplaced perceptions about death. As with younger children, use clear, concrete and honest answers. Make sure children have the opportunity to interact with the dying person and offer choices about how they can offer care. Support parents so they are better able to model healthy coping behaviors for their children.

Pre-teens. Pre-teens are more likely to understand that death is final and happens to everyone. They may have fewer questions about death, often preferring to avoid talking about it. While they may be reluctant to open up, they may experience anxiety, anger or guilt. Some may overreact emotionally or have delayed emotional reactions. Some may withdraw from their friends or engage in acting out behaviors such as fighting.

How to help: Help pre-teens by encouraging them to talk about their thoughts and feelings. Encourage them to use healthy ways to vent their emotional and energy. Be direct and honest, giving factual information about death and dying. Support parents by listening to the challenges they may face with pre-teens and helping them with ways to provide support.

Additional Resources About Children and Teens

Caring Connections

Provides resources to engage communities around pediatric end of life care at www.caringinfo/community/PediatricOutreach.htm.

Helping Children Cope With the Loss of a Loved One: A Guide for Grownups, by William C. Kroen; Free Spirit Publishing, 1996

Advice for adults helping a child cope with death. Includes stories of real children and their families and explains how children from infancy to age 18 think about and react to death.

How Do We Tell the Children? A Step-by-Step Guide for Helping Children Two to Teen Cope When Someone Dies, by Dan Schaefer and Christine Lyons; Newmarket Press, 1993

Practical advice to help adults talk to children of all ages about death, formatted for different developmental ages.

Talking About Death: A Dialogue Between Parent and Child, by Earl Grollman; Beacon Press, 1990

Review of ways to talk with children about the death of loved ones that includes modeled conversations, age-appropriate guidelines and a complete list of resources.

Additional Resources For Children and Teens

Deal With It: The Bible on Death and Dying, **by Ann Bach and Rebecca Slough; Generation Why Bible Studies, Faith and Life Publishers, 1999**

Series of five sessions discusses the reality of death, questions of despair, depression and suicide designed to help youth death with grief and deepen their faith.

The Fall of Freddie the Leaf: A Story of Life for All Age, **by Leo Buscaglia; Slack Inc., 1982**

"Why do we have to die? Where do we go when we die?" This allegory addresses these questions in a way that helps children and adults appreciate the changes of nature and accept death. *Reading level: ages 4 to 8*

In My World: Official Life Journal, **by Linda Lazar and Bonnie Crawford; The Centering Corporation, 1999**

Workbook for adolescents facing life-threatening illness. It lets them fill the blanks about things like "All about me," "The things I have done," "If my future were left up to me to plan," and more.

Lifetimes: The Beautiful Way to Explain Death to Children, **by Bryan Mellonie and Robert Ingpen; Bantam Books, 1983**

Simple language and colorful illustrations help small children understand the natural cycle of life: birth, growth, aging, death, emphasizing that dying is as much a part of living as being born. *Reading level: ages 9 to 12*

The Next Place, **by Warren Hanson; Walden House Press, 1997**

A beautifully illustrated and inspirational book describing the feelings, colors and timelessness of "the next place." *Reading level: ages 4 to 8*

On the Wings of a Butterfly: A Story About Life and Death, **by Marilyn Maple; Parenting Press, 1992**

The story of a young child dying of cancer who finds comfort and support in her friendship with a caterpillar preparing to become a butterfly. They share their fears and questions about the unknown together. *Reading level: ages 9 to 12*

Sargeant's Heaven, **by Icy Frantz; Franz and Weld, 2008**

Story inspired by the author's three young sons after the death of their youngest brother. See www.sargeantsheaven.com.

Straight Talk About Death for Teenagers: How to Cope With Losing Someone You Love, **by Earl Grollman; Beacon Press, 1993**

Geared for teenagers, written in a straightforward yet sensitive manner. *Reading level: young adult*

Water Bugs and Dragonflies: Explaining Death to Young Children, **by Doris Stickney; Pilgrim Press, 1982**

A simple story from nature ends with a short prayer for the person who has died.

Teenagers. Teenagers understand death and may experience denial, anxiety, anger, depression or any other emotion connected with death of someone they love. Some may repress their feelings or act indifferent. They are more likely to talk with their friends than with their parents about death and dying. Some will ask spiritual questions and begin a search for meaning. Some will engage in risky behavior with alcohol, drugs, fast driving and other attempts to test their own mortality.

How to help: Help teenagers by being available to them without pushing. Encourage the open discussion of thoughts, feelings and the search for meaning. While it may be fine to tolerate regressive or some acting out behavior, help them with impulse control when it comes to risky behavior. Because they are more like to talk with peers, offer opportunities for them to talk with friend their age if possible.

Incorporating End of Life Into Worship

Many faith communities focus their attention on death in worship at funerals and memorial services, after death has occurred. However, few congregations regularly weave end of life issues into worship, helping people integrate the spiritual and theological implications into their beliefs and practices.

Incorporating end of life matters into worship helps people connect the realities of this season of life with their relationship with God. And doing so helps create a congregational culture that is honest and open about the realities of life and death and one that extends circles of care to members as they live with end of life issues.

As you plan to support people around end of life through worship, use the general recommendations on worship found in the chapter Creating Unbroken Circles of Care; then consider incorporating the ideas and resources mentioned in this section.

Special Worship Services

It is important for faith communities to offer worship for people at the end of life as well as for all congregation members. Some ideas for special services, both with the individual dying person and in groups honoring him or her, are discussed below.

Vigils and rituals at the bedside. In many traditions, vigils—which may involve prayer, reading, talking, singing, healing touch and performing rituals—offer spiritual presence for a person who is dying.

For example, in Roman Catholic tradition, rituals may include performing an unction of the sick or praying the litany of the saints. Some Protestant traditions also practice anointing before a death. In Jewish tradition, dying people may wish to recite the prayer

The Lord is my shepherd,
I shall not want.

He makes me lie down
in green pastures;
he leads me beside still waters;

He restores my soul.
He leads me in right paths
for his name's sake.

Even though I walk
through the darkest valley,
I fear no evil;
for you are with me;
your rod and your staff—
they comfort me.

You prepare a table before me
in the presence of my enemies;
you anoint my head with oil;
my cup overflows.

Surely goodness and mercy
shall follow me all the days
of my life,
and I shall dwell in the house of
the Lord my whole life long.

PSALM 23, NRSV

of confession known as the Vidui. In Muslim tradition, the dying person, known as the Muhtadar, and others may recite the two Articles of Faith known as the Kalimas. (To learn more, see the Sacred Dying Foundation's website: www. sacreddying.org.)

When people are dying and unable to attend worship, consider creative ways to take sacred space to them. Create a portable worship kit including a few items such as a small banner, an altar cloth, an object from the worship space, a prayer book, a candle or other sacred objects.

When clergy or congregational caregivers visit, items from the kit may be used to prepare sacred space for worship, communion or prayer. The knowledge that these objects are part of the worshiping life of the congregation can help members feel connected when they are away. (For an annotated list of resources, including the rituals and traditions of diverse denominations and faith traditions, see the Duke Institute on Care at the End of Life's website: www.iceol.duke.edu.)

To Each His or Her Own

Knowing how to pray with others when death nears is difficult because what gives comfort and ease to one dying person can cause anxiety and unease for another. Such was the case when a beloved pastor of mine was dying. Although he was conscious, he could neither see nor speak. One of his priest friends and I stayed the night with him. At a moment when it appeared he was close to his last breath, his friend and I began singing church songs such as "Be Not Afraid" and "On Eagle's Wings."

As I gazed upon the pastor's face, I sensed the need for quiet, remembering what he had once told me about wanting silence in his house for his morning prayer. So I leaned down close to his ear and asked, "Would you like us to stop singing? If yes, squeeze my hand." His response, even in his weakened state, was to nearly squash my fingers!

Another time I was with a young man dying of AIDS who wanted the opposite of silence. He asked that classical music be played continually in his room during his final days. Because each person has his or her own needs when approaching death, we cannot presume that one or two church rituals will best assist every dying person.

ADAPTED FROM "GO IN PEACE: RITUALS FOR THE DYING," BY JOYCE RUPP: WWW.JOYCERUPP.COM.

Rituals and vigils supporting people who are dying. Dying people may not wish to have a crowd of people with them as they approach the end of life. However, even when it's not possible or preferable to be in the dying person's presence, faith community members may show support by gathering for a prayer vigil or service at the congregation's place of worship.

For example, one woman living with breast cancer received care for two years from an eight-member support team organized by her faith community. When her illness shifted so that she was actively dying, she did not have room or energy for the whole team to gather with her. Anxious to provide some kind of support, members of the caregiving team gathered at their church for a time of prayer. They told their dying friend they would be gathering as a way to support her and each other. Surrounded by music, candles and prayer, they walked a labyrinth in her honor. Later, they learned she died during that time.

By offering opportunities for members to gather on behalf of others who are dying, congregations honor the end of life journey, show support for the person dying and family members and have an opportunity to support one another.

Hospice Sabbath services. Hospice Sabbath, observed during National Hospice Month in November, is an opportunity to recognize people who are near the end of life. During Hospice Sabbath, faith communities may pray for hospice patients and families and all people facing life-limiting illness. Alternatively, there may be one community service bringing together people of different faith traditions. Often organized by hospices or end of life care coalitions, these groups often provide sample prayers and poems and offer staff and volunteer speakers. Though faith communities are not usually the organizers, they can support and encourage Hospice Sabbaths in their communities. (To find out whether such a service exists in your area, contact your local hospice agencies.)

Weekly Worship

As emphasized, few faith communities integrate reflection on end of life issues into their regular cycles of worship. However, there are a number of ways congregations can include topics related to death and dying into worship.

- Scripture: Include scriptures that address death and dying as part of your service planning. Do not avoid difficult passages, but include them as part of your worship when appropriate.

- **Readings, poems, liturgies and prayers:** Incorporate readings, poems, liturgies and prayers from other sources into your worship. You may choose to use some of the poems and prayers included in this toolkit, including the one below. Following a member's death, if the person or family requested a special reading as part of the funeral or memorial service, you may include that reading, poem or prayer in a later worship service, recognizing the connection with the person who died.

- **Children's sermons:** Children's books are a natural starting place for crafting children's sermons related to death. (See the books described on pages 57, 85 and 111 for some good examples.)

- **Personal stories and testimonies:** Invite members to share their own stories of caring for others at the end of life as part of worship. Encourage people to talk about their struggles and difficulties as well as their experiences of inspiration and hope.

- **Sermons and homilies:** Draw on scripture, books, movies, personal experiences, the deaths of church members and other sources to integrate death and dying into sermons or homilies. Address theological issues and concerns that people may face but be afraid to discuss or explore. By doing so, you help members to talk about thoughts and feelings that may be difficult for them to express.

- **Visual arts:** Banners and sacred art can be used to remind members of the sacredness of the end of life journey. Consider creating a banner or quilt to be hung in the sanctuary for a set period of time, such as a week, after a member dies.

Prayer of Death and Eternal Life

Eternal God, who sees all things,
we pray for those who hope for what is unseen. We pray especially
for the elderly and their caregivers and for those at the end of life.
We pray for doctors, nurses, hospice workers and friends who accompany
families at such times.

We remember those who share the final moments by the bedside
of a loved one and seek your mercy in the threshold between life and death.
May they encounter the abundance of your grace in such moments.
May the death of your faithful ones inspire us to live toward the hope
that is unseen, that eternal hope for which you have made us.
Lord in your mercy, hear our prayer.

FROM "PRAYERS OF THE PEOPLE," DUKE CHAPEL SUNDAY MORNING WORSHIP SERVICE, DURHAM, NORTH CAROLINA

Additional Resources About End of Life in Worship

Beliefnet

Includes an online library of prayers from different faith traditions for times of illness, death, aging, comfort, healing, hope, strength and courage, loneliness and other end of life situations. For more, go to www.beliefnet.com.

***Healing Liturgies for the Seasons of Life,* by Abigail Rian Evans; Westminster John Knox, 2004**

A specialist in bioethics and health ministries explores ways healing is available throughout life through liturgical services, sacraments and rites. This resource features liturgies for injury, illness, death, separation, retirement and other major life events, from a variety of traditions.

Ritualwell

Website focused on Jewish ritual innovations for holidays and lifecycles as well as time-honored Jewish customs. It encourages creativity in making or adapting rituals that meet personal, religious and aesthetic requirements. Includes rituals and prayers surrounding "healing and hard times," "growing older" and "death and grief." For more, go to wwww.ritualwell.org.

***Sacred Dying: Creating Rituals for Embracing the End of Life,* by Megory Anderson; Da Capo Press, 2003**

Handbook for creating a dignified, peaceful and more sacred end to life that includes a section with prayers and poems from various traditions. It shows ways to create and personalize rituals for dying people to bring peace, reconciliation and acceptance. Discusses all aspects of this final transition, including how to help dying people with "unfinished business," massage to help the dying release his or her body and use of music for life review.

***Speaking to Silence: New Rites for Christian Worship and Healing,* by Janet S. Peterman; Westminster John Knox Press, 2007**

Offers reflection on the significance of rituals and introduces new rituals, including rituals for use at home, at church or in the community. Describes a seven-step process for creating new rituals and suggests ways to adapt existing worship materials for use in new settings.

The Uniqueness of Grief 90

The Purpose of Grief and Mourning 91

    Acknowledging the Death 91

    Experiencing the Pain 91

    Making Sense of the Death 91

    Remembering the Deceased 92

    Adjusting to a New Life 92

    Relearning the World 92

Reactions to Grief 92

    The Stages of Grief Theory 92

    Factors in Processing Grief 92

    Reconciling Grief 94

Traumatic Grief 95

Children, Teens and Grief 95

Congregational Action Planning 96

Grief Education 97

    Educational Sessions 97

    A Grief Series 100

Congregational Care 101

    Support Immediately Following Death 101

    Extended Support 104

    Spiritual Support 106

    Grief Support Teams 107

    Grief Support Groups 107

    Support for Grieving Children 110

    Support for Grieving Teens 111

Support Following Traumatic Death 112

    Accidental Death or Disaster 112

    Homicide 113

    Suicide 113

    Death of a Child 114

Incorporating Grief Into Worship 115

    Funerals and Memorial Services 116

    Services for Grieving People 117

    Services Recognizing Grief 119

    Creative Rituals for Grief Support 120

YESTERDAY'S PAIN

In the godforsaken,

obscene quicksand of life,

there is a deafening alleluia

rising from the souls

of those who weep,

and of those who weep with those who weep.

If you watch, you will see

the hand of God

putting the stars back in their skies

one by one.

POET ANN WEEMS

To provide feedback
on this toolkit, go to
www.iceol.duke.edu.

Grief is a deeply personal experience—a normal and natural response to death and loss. It affects every aspect of a person's being: body, mind, heart and spirit. And grief often lasts for months to years, profoundly changing the way people understand life, relationships and the world around them. It is a season of life that can bring pain and suffering as well as healing and transformation.

Unfortunately, American culture often misinterprets grief and denies its impact. Many people believe that grief is "just an emotion" that lasts for a few days or weeks and then goes away. Following a significant loss, people often expect others to quickly resume their lives.

Even faith communities commonly underestimate the impact and duration of grief. While congregations often respond to grief by offering funeral and memorial services and some support following death, few of them help members understand the dynamics of grief before it comes—and fewer still extend helpful grief support and community presence throughout the whole season of grief.

A key step is for clergy and lay leaders to learn more about the purpose, dynamics and impact of grief, which can then empower them to teach others about its true nature and to create ministries that meet people where they are throughout the grieving process.

The Uniqueness of Grief

Each person's grief experience is unique—and it changes, depending on the circumstances and relationships involved. For example, grief related to losing a spouse is different from grief over losing a child or a sibling.

One of the challenges grieving people face is that others often do not understand the significance of their loss. Sometimes others diminish a loss by saying things such as: "At least she lived a long life; you had her for so many years." And people often compare their own grief to another person's, thinking they have it harder or easier, and worrying that their own reactions are inadequate or unnatural. However, because grief is unique and individual, there is no way to fully understand what another person is experiencing. An important truth in grief support is: "The worst kind of grief is the one you are going through. The worst kind of grief is your own."

To support others through grief, it is essential to understand the wide range of possible reactions to it.

Semantics of Grief

The following words that relate to grief are often used interchangeably. However, each term has a distinctive meaning in this toolkit. As you learn more about grief and prepare to teach others about it, it's also helpful to sharpen your grief vocabulary.

Bereavement: The root of the term means "shorn off" or "torn up." It is the period after a loss during which grief is experienced and mourning occurs. Bereavement is usually associated with a sense of being disrupted or deprived of something or someone.

Grief: An internal reaction to loss that affects every aspect of life. Reactions to grief may be physical, behavioral, emotional, spiritual or social. The experience of grief may extend for months or years.

Mourning: The outward sign of the inward grief experience. For example, lowering a flag, wearing a black armband, participating in a funeral or memorial service and the Jewish tradition of sitting shiva are all mourning rituals.

Lament: A particular kind of mourning. In many faith traditions, lament is an expression of grief through scripture, song or poem. The psalms are perhaps the most familiar examples of scriptural lament. In some traditions, laments include keening and wailing.

The Purpose of Grief and Mourning

Whether grieving begins before or after a death, its purpose is to help people process the loss and find a way to heal. A few of the many facets of the experience of grief are described below.

Acknowledging the Death

When someone dies, the death may not seem real to the survivors. Some people avoid talking about the loss; others immerse themselves in work or dealing with details of the final arrangements to keep from thinking about the person who died.

The survivors often experience some form of shock—which often triggers reactions such as disorientation, disbelief, numbing or feeling as if they are in a daze. Shock is a mechanism that protects people so that they can cope with the loss at their own paces. While most survivors experience shock following death, people who have anticipated a death due to prolonged illness tend to move through shock to accepting the reality of the loss more quickly because they have already experienced some grief. When death is unexpected or sudden, shock is often more acute and lasts longer. As shock wears off, survivors begin to acknowledge the loss—coming to understand that the person has, in fact, died.

Experiencing the Pain

As the reality of the death sinks in, people may have a wide range of thoughts, feelings, spiritual questions and physical symptoms that will intensify before they subside. Because this painful period often sets in several weeks or months after a death occurs, the most intense grief reactions are often just beginning about the time that grieving

Give sorrow words; the grief that does not speak whispers the o'er-fraught heart and bids it break.

William Shakespeare

survivors are being urged by those around them to "start moving on." This may be because people who are less affected by the death are ready to move on themselves and are not prepared to offer empathetic support for those who are more affected—those who have a wide range of thoughts, emotions, spiritual questions and physical symptoms to experience.

Faith communities, too, often underestimate how long it takes to process grief, expecting people to move through it much more quickly than they are able. As a result, the grief support congregations offer often subsides about the time a survivor's actual grief experience becomes the most intense. Without effective congregational support, people who are grieving will feel as if the faith community has left them behind.

Making Sense of the Death

Making meaning of a death is part of the process of integrating reality into a person's way of seeing the world. And so it often follows that the more senseless the death seems to a person, the more the grieving process will involve a search for meaning. This does not necessarily mean the grieving person will decide that the death of a loved one was justified or served a higher purpose, especially when the death was tragic. But it can mean creating something good and lasting in response.

Anticipatory Grief

People living with illness may experience many types of losses—including loss of mobility, memory, hearing, vision and sense of identity. Losses may come one at a time, in waves or all at once.

By themselves, these losses bring grief. They also often cause people to look ahead and anticipate losses to come. Sometimes anticipated losses are incremental ones, such as loss of independence. Ultimately, at the heart of anticipatory grief is an awareness of death.

Anticipatory grief can affect an individual living with illness and also those connected with that person.

As with all forms of grief, anticipatory grief may affect people physically, emotionally, spiritually and socially. Signs of anticipatory grief may include sadness, anger, depression, mood swings, denial, forgetfulness, confusion, sleep disturbance, fatigue and weight gain or loss.

A hallmark of anticipatory grief is a sense of anxiety and dread. Individuals and family members see death coming but do not know how and when it will occur. The sense of "not knowing" can be especially difficult.

Because this form of grief is not often discussed in our culture, congregations can help by supporting members so that they will be able to talk about their anticipatory grief with pastoral caregivers rather than hide it. By encouraging members to take advantage of congregational caregiving, support groups and counseling offered by hospice and other organizations, congregations help people experiencing anticipatory grief cope more effectively with the losses they face.

Remembering the Deceased

Grief helps people find ways to remember those who have died. While a funeral or memorial service may play a role in this process, people often seek different ways to remember over time. These may be small, personal gestures—such as telling stories, sharing photo albums, humming or singing songs or placing certain objects in an important place. Or they may be more public demonstrations, such as planting a garden or creating a memorial. While there may be many signs of remembering, the heart of the task is for grieving people to find ways to keep the deceased person in their memories and in their lives.

Adjusting to a New Life

Adjusting after another's death may require a grieving survivor to make major life changes, such as finding a new place to live, obtaining a new source of income or raising children alone. But small changes such as balancing a checkbook, preparing meals, going to worship or making decisions alone may also seem overwhelming. This adjustment phase of the grief journey can be distressing and can bring painful feelings of loneliness and inadequacy. The challenge is to begin to function again in daily life without the other person.

Relearning the World

As people work through grieving, they reach a point at which they have renewed energy and interest in new relationships, activities and ways of being. These feelings may be different from those they experienced previously, reflecting the changes that come through the healing process. Some people may join or rejoin a faith community. Relearning the world and rediscovering life is one of the healthy results of the grieving process.

Reactions to Grief

While there is no exact timeframe for the acute phase of grief to progress from beginning to end, the process may take months or even years. During this time, people experience a wide range of symptoms, feelings, thoughts, beliefs and social interactions.

People experiencing grief and those around them are often not aware of all the ways grief can be expressed. Many people wonder if the grief they are experiencing is normal. Left to wonder whether their grief reactions are normal, people may feel isolated and alone. To support others through grief, it is essential to understand the wide range of possible reactions as a first step toward helping them.

The Stages of Grief Theory

The theory that grief includes five distinct stages is the most widely known and taught model for grief support. That model was introduced by Elisabeth Kübler-Ross in her 1969 book *On Death and Dying*. Kübler-Ross summarized these stages as:

- Denial. "This can't be happening."
- Anger. "Why did you leave me? If only..."
- Bargaining. "If you will just..."
- Depression. "I'm so sad, so alone. Why bother?"
- Acceptance. "It's going to be OK."

Since Kübler-Ross published her groundbreaking work, an entire field of literature has emerged that seeks to describe grief. Many leaders in the field now describe grief as a widely variable process with no single timeline and progression.

Factors in Processing Grief

While grief has often been described as occurring in stages, many people

experience it in cycles, bursts or waves. In fact, some describe grief as a rollercoaster experience filled with uncertainty and change. While the stage theory can be helpful for understanding grief, it is also crucial to take into account the factors that may affect a person's grief experience.

Type of Death

How a person dies influences how survivors grieve. In particular, sudden death, accidental death, violent death and suicide allow no time for people to prepare for the loss—and the potential for shock and disbelief may increase, along with the level of disorientation, anger, loss and depression. (Later sections of this chapter address how to support people who are grieving each of these types of death.)

Relationship With the Deceased

The type of relationship between the deceased and grieving survivor also has an impact on the grief experience. For example, the death of a child is significantly different from the death of a spouse. The nature and quality of the relationship also matters: The more attached the person was emotionally, cognitively, spiritually, socially and financially, the more intense the grief response is likely to be. Having "unfinished business" with the person who died such as unresolved guilt or not having the opportunity to "say goodbye" will also affect grief and the grieving process.

Past Experience

While each experience is different, people who have effectively worked through grief before may recognize the dynamics when they experience it again. Some people develop personal insights that help them,

COMMON REACTIONS DURING THE GRIEVING PROCESS

Physical & behavioral reactions

- fatigue
- exhaustion
- lack of strength
- agitation
- crying
- sleep disturbances
- appetite disturbances
- decreased immune system
- tightness in the throat
- hair loss
- acting out or impulsive behavior
- searching behavior
- restless and disorganized activity
- decreased effectiveness
- decreased productivity

Emotional reactions

- sadness
- sorrow
- anguish
- anger
- anxiety or panic
- fear
- guilt
- feeling out of control
- irritability
- impatience
- regret
- depression
- loneliness
- abandonment
- insecurity
- relief
- peace
- hope

Cognitive reactions

- disbelief
- confusion
- lack of focus
- lost sense of purpose
- disillusionment
- feelings of inadequacy
- questioning
- decreased interest in life
- preoccupation with the person who died
- focus on what is missing
- loss or change of identity
- thoughts about "going crazy"
- generalized thoughts of suicide

Spiritual reactions

- questioning meaning and purpose
- questioning faith
- feeling abandoned by God
- feeling angry at God
- feeling disconnected from God
- feeling disconnected from a faith community
- sense of guilt or regret about things done or undone
- feelings of brokenness
- loss of hope

Social reactions

- lack of interest in others
- disinterest in usual activities
- withdrawal from others
- loss of patterns of social interaction
- sense of detachment or alienation from others
- dependency on others
- avoidance of being alone
- jealousy of others who have not had a loss

such as: "For me, coping with grief includes learning to expect the unexpected." Others who have not worked through previous losses may relive them again when another one comes. In such cases, grief may be cumulative and compounded.

Personality of the Survivor

People who have more affective personalities often lead with their feelings and more readily feel the pain of loss and are more apt to discuss it. Those with more cognitive personalities often lead with their thoughts and may focus first on meaning before turning to their affective side. How a person adapts to change and transition also makes a difference.

Reconciling Grief

A couple of specialized types of grief are discussed below. But for all grievers, the tasks, stages and cycles of grief and mourning help "reconcile" loss—that is, come to terms with it and integrate it into their everyday lives.

Eventually, the grief process will help the person remember and miss the one who has died without experiencing the acute pain, confusion and disorientation of the loss. However, acute grief may recur at different times throughout a person's lifetime, even decades after a death. This renewed grief often occurs less often and for briefer periods as time goes on.

Beyond Grief and Gender: A Matter of Style

Misunderstanding about the different ways people grieve can create tension within couples, families and congregations. Often the misunderstanding has been typecast as the difference between "women who grieve and men who don't." However, much more is now known about how different people grieve.

Early studies that attempted to address the perceived differences between men and women claimed that men "kept themselves busy" to avoid grief and women, on the other hand, "dealt with their grief" by expressing emotions.

It has become clear, however, that the different ways people experience grief are not tied to gender, but to "grief styles." Recognizing that both men and women have traditionally defined masculine and feminine qualities, grief theorists Terry Martin and Kenneth Doka move beyond gender stereotypes to discuss "instrumental" and "intuitive" grief styles.

Instrumental grief is cognitive, thought-oriented and action-oriented. It usually remains private and focuses on the future. Instrumental grievers lead with problem solving, planning or hands-on activities. For example, instrumental grievers may focus on activities such as settling an estate, creating a memorial, volunteering, writing a book or planting a garden.

Intuitive grief leads with emotion and may include expressing strong feelings connected with the loss. Intuitive grievers often find comfort in talking about what they are feeling and listening to others. For example, intuitive grievers may value telling their story again and again, participating in a group with other grievers and sharing their experience with others.

While one style typically leads, no one person is exclusively instrumental or intuitive. Instrumental grievers experience emotion and intuitive griever can be action and activity oriented in their grief. Understanding your own grief style and the styles of your family and friends will help as you experience your own grief and as you thoughtfully support others through grief and loss.

To learn more, see *Men Don't Cry... Women Do: Transcending Gender Stereotypes of Grief*, by Terry L. Martin and Kenneth J. Doka; Routledge, 1999.

Additional Resources on Grief, Generally

Grief, Dying and Death: Clinical Interventions for Caregivers, **by Therese A Rando; Research Press, 1984**

Includes topics such as anticipatory grief, post-death mourning, the stress of grief and grief reactions and their causes are analyzed. Special attention on grief caused by the death of a child or spouse, death by suicide and children's grief.

How We Grieve: Relearning the World, **by Thomas Attig; Oxford University Press, 1996**

Represents grieving as an active process of that transforms the fabric of life— including relearning things and places and relationships with others.

Traumatic Grief

Sometimes grief lingers and becomes more debilitating over time. Frequently described in the literature as "complicated grief," this form of grief includes major depression, anxiety disorders, signs of post-traumatic stress syndrome and other long-term affects. As a result, some grief theorists now use the term "traumatic grief" to describe this condition. As many as one in five people who are grieving may experience some form of it.

There are a number of factors that can put people at higher risk for these forms of grief—including suffering recent multiple losses, having low self-esteem or health problems.

While some people show clear signs of traumatic grief such as severe depression or suicidal ideation, it often goes unnoticed. Some signs of traumatic grief may include:

- extreme and ongoing difficulty acknowledging the loss

- persistent and disturbing thoughts or beliefs about the death

- physical complaints that persist or existing complaints that worsen

- marked, sustained sleep difficulties

- decreased ability to work

- extended withdrawal from family and friends

- persistent and prolonged distress, guilt, self-blame or despair, and

- very limited or no interest in life.

It can be difficult even for professionals to assess traumatic grief, especially early on. However, it is important for clergy and lay leaders to know the signs of complicated

grief and be prepared to make a referral to a qualified grief counselor for an assessment. For people who are experiencing traumatic grief, formal grief counseling can make a significant difference.

Children, Teens and Grief

Well-meaning adults will sometimes try to "protect" children from illness, death and grief. However, this often has the opposite effect from the one intended: It teaches that death and grief are not acceptable and excludes children from grief support.

As with adults, grief affects children physically, behaviorally, emotionally, mentally and spiritually. However, because children are still developing, some of they ways they express grief will appear different from adult grief. By understanding this, you will be better prepared to offer children helpful support as they experience grief and as they learn how to cope with losses in the future.

Young children. Children experiencing grief may have decreased activity levels, suppressed appetites or sleep disturbances. They may become irritable, often because of changes to routine. Preschool and school-age children may grieve in spurts—talking clearly about intense emotions one moment and playing the next. They often ask the same questions over and over. These young children may experience either increased

or decreased appetite and activity levels. They may increase attention-seeking behavior, demonstrate violent behavior as they play or withdraw from social interaction. They may lose sleep or have vivid dreams when they do sleep.

How to help. Receiving clear and direct answers to questions, having a consistent routine, getting opportunities to play and having caring support from adults all help younger children cope.

Older children. From age eight or so, children may talk more about their grief and express anger, sadness or confusion. They may ask lots of questions about how people die and what happens to them. Older children usually develop the capacity for mourning and become interested in what other people think about death and grief. They may begin having problems at school, lose interest in friends and act out at school or at home.

How to help. These children benefit from opportunities to talk as well as from having time alone. Having choices, expressing emotions and talking though their questions all make a positive difference. Play and exercise can also help.

Pre-teens and teens. Children at this age tend to experience the full range of grief reactions. They can exhibit strong emotions—from anger to sadness to denial. These emerging adults tend to be more likely to talk with friends and people outside their families about their grief than with parents. They may act out, reject former beliefs and teachings and become angry toward their parents and other authorities.

How to help. Demonstrating respect for the grief young people experience, offering thoughtful options and choices, providing a supportive and listening ear and encouraging them to explore their grief healthy ways will make a difference.

(See resources below for additional tips on how to support grieving children of all ages.)

Congregational Action Planning

The chapter titled Creating Unbroken Circles of Care will help you discover general approaches to leadership development, education, congregational care, worship, communications and supportive and accessible space. This chapter provides models and resources specific to creating unbroken circles around grief.

Additional Resources for Grieving Children and Teens

The Fall of Freddie the Leaf: A Story of Life for All Ages, **by Leo Buscaglia; Slack Inc., 1982**

Addresses death and afterlife in a way that helps children and adults appreciate the changes of nature and accept the season of death. *Reading level: ages 4 to 8*

Lifetimes: Beginnings and Endings With Lifetimes in Between: A Beautiful Way to Explain Death to Children, **by Bryan Mellonie and Robert Ingpen; Institute of Pacific Studies, 1991**

Simple language and colorful illustrations help small children understand the natural cycle of life: birth, growth, aging and death. *Reading level: ages 3 to 6*

Part of Me Died, Too, **by Virginia Lynn Fry; Dutton Children's Books, 1995**

Ten studies of children and teenagers in mourning. Includes "survival strategies" that outline journal exercises and other projects to help channel grief. *Reading level: ages 10 and up*

When Dinosaurs Die: A Guide to Understanding Death, **by Laurie Krasny Brown and Marc Brown; Little Brown Publishing, 1996**

Addresses children's fears and curiosity head-on, and in a largely secular fashion, by answering some very basic questions: "Why does someone die?" "What does dead mean?" "What comes after death?" Other questions deal with emotions, and there's a section about death customs. *Reading level: ages 4 to 8*

Help in Your Own Front Yard: Community Resources

Community organizations can be helpful partners as you learn more about grief support and offer programs and support for your congregation members. Seek out professional partners in community settings such as those mentioned below.

Hospices. Hospices are required to offer grief support services following the death of a patient. Many offer grief support groups for non-hospice families as well. Hospices often have bereavement counselors on staff, many of whom are social workers or chaplains. These professionals can work with you in planning educational programs for lay leaders or congregational members. Hospices may also have a collection of grief support resources you may be able to access. Go to www.nhpco.org to locate hospices in your area.

Hospital chaplaincy departments. Some hospital chaplaincy departments offer bereavement services for hospital patients and staff. They may also partner with you as you develop grief support programs. The hospital may also have a freestanding bereavement program that can be a valuable resource.

Children and teen grief support programs. Some communities have programs developed specifically to support children, teens and their parents who are living with grief. Many programs are part of hospice organizations. However, others may be part of school counseling programs and other organizations. Programs may offer grief support camps, evening programs and other services for children and teens. Whether you are learning more about children and grief or planning a program, staff in these programs may be helpful. To find these programs, contact a local hospice.

Funeral homes. Many funeral homes provide grief support materials and may have staff trained in grief support.

Traumatic death specialists. Organizations that respond to traumatic death situations may include violence prevention groups, suicide prevention groups, government organizations that respond to critical incidents and others.

Therapists, mental health counselors, licensed clinical social workers. Many mental health professionals have developed specialties in grief support and may be helpful resources for you in your learning process and program planning. You should be able locate them through an Internet search of "grief therapy" and your locale.

Grief Education

By offering grief education, you equip members to better understand grief when it comes and to be more receptive to pastoral and congregational support during their grieving period and will honor it as a part of worship and the spiritual journey.

Review the chapter Creating Unbroken Circles of Care as you begin planning. Then use the tools and resources in this section to develop your educational programs about grief.

Educational Sessions

Whether you offer grief education sessions during a designated adult education time such as Sunday School, or create a time such as a weekday evening program, the following model sessions may serve as a helpful guides. They may be used as written or adapted. In addition, as you plan additional sessions, they offer a format you can adapt to other grief-related topics.

1   Educational Session 1: The Spiritual Journey of Grief

Grief may be one of life's most challenging and difficult transitions. It also raises significant spiritual questions for many people of faith. Although grief can bring sorrow and suffering, it can also bring spiritual growth and transformation.

This session explores the spiritual aspects of grief, discusses ways it may challenge faith and how it can also offer hope.

1. Opening: 5 minutes

Select a poem or quote or offer a prayer to begin. You may wish to use one of devotional resources in this toolkit or select your own.

2. A Story of Grief: 5 minutes

Select a story of grief from scripture or a spiritual source. For example, the story of Naomi from the first chapter of the book of Ruth brings up the loss of a spouse and other family members, loss of basic subsistence and threat of the loss of family relationships. As a result, Naomi changes her name to Mara, meaning "bitter," and says that God has dealt harshly with her. Read or provide the story. If you choose, provide some background on the culture of the time and the economic challenges widows faced as a way to help participants understand Naomi's losses.

3. Reflection on the Story of Grief: 10 minutes

Ask participants to work in pairs or small groups to discuss the following questions:

- What losses did Naomi experience?

- How did it affect her relationship with the people around her?

- How did it affect her relationship with God?

- What feelings toward God did Naomi express?

- What thoughts did Naomi express about God?

- How do you feel about how Naomi's grief affected her relationship with God?

4. Spiritual Reactions to Grief: 10 minutes

Use the introductory information and additional resources listed in this chapter to introduce possible spiritual reactions to grief, including:

- questioning meaning and purpose

- questioning faith

- feeling abandoned by God

- feeling angry toward God

- feeling disconnected from God

- feeling disconnected from faith community

- sensing guilt or regret about things done or undone

- feelings of brokenness, and

- losing hope.

Reinforce the idea that these reactions do not necessarily indicate a loss of faith, but rather a quest for meaning and an experience of spiritual change and growth.

4. Exploring Spiritual Reactions to Grief: 15 minutes

Ask participants to return to their pairs or small groups and to recall a time when they experienced a loss.

Discuss the following questions:

- What was the situation you are remembering?

- How did the loss affect you spiritually?

- Did you experience one of the common reactions to spiritual grief?

- How did you feel about your reaction at the time?

- Was there anyone with whom you were able to discuss this?

- What helped you move through this sense of loss?

5. Discuss Spiritual Support: 10 minutes

As a large group, discuss questions such as:

- What do these spiritual reactions to grief say about how faith communities can support people through grief?

- What has your own experience with spiritual reactions to grief taught you about how your faith community can support you through grief?

- What can our faith community do to support people spiritually through grief?

Use the insights you gain from this discussion to help inform your congregational care planning.

6. Closing: 5 minutes

You may choose to close with a prayer or a reading or by offering participants the opportunity to spontaneously offer a word of hope.

GOD'S MIGHTY DEEDS RECALLED

Psalm 77, verses 1-20

1 I cry aloud to God, aloud to God, that he may hear me.

2 In the day of my trouble I seek the Lord; in the night my hand is stretched out without wearying; my soul refuses to be comforted.

3 I think of God, and I moan; I meditate, and my spirit faints. Selah

4 You keep my eyelids from closing; I am so troubled that I cannot speak.

5 I consider the days of old, and remember the years of long ago.

6 I commune with my heart in the night; I meditate and search my spirit:

7 "Will the Lord spurn forever, and never again be favorable?

8 Has his steadfast love ceased forever? Are his promises at an end for all time?

9 Has God forgotten to be gracious? Has he in anger shut up his compassion?" Selah

10 And I say, "It is my grief that the right hand of the Most High has changed."

11 I will call to mind the deeds of the Lord; I will remember your wonders of old.

12 I will meditate on all your work, and muse on your mighty deeds.

13 Your way, O God, is holy. What god is so great as our God?

14 You are the God who works wonders; you have displayed your might among the peoples.

15 With your strong arm you redeemed your people, the descendants of Jacob and Joseph. Selah

16 When the waters saw you, O God, when the waters saw you, they were afraid; the very deep trembled.

17 The clouds poured out water; the skies thundered; your arrows flashed on every side.

18 The crash of your thunder was in the whirlwind; your lightnings lit up the world; the earth trembled and shook.

19 Your way was through the sea, your path, through the mighty waters; yet your footprints were unseen.

20 You led your people like a flock by the hand of Moses and Aaron.

A lament is a spiritual expression of mourning through scripture, song or poem. The psalms, a common example of lament, offer a tremendous resource for support as people of faith live with grief. Laments are addressed to God and traditionally include a complaint or grievance, a request for God to act and an expression of confidence and gratitude that God will hear the lament.

This session explores one of the psalms of lament and focuses on how it fits into our lives and community of faith.

1. Opening: 5 minutes

Make copies of Psalm 77: 1-20, on the previous page, and begin by asking participants to read it alone or together.

2. Discussing the Patterns of Lament:
   10 minutes

Open with a brief discussion of the tradition of lament in the psalms. Nearly half of all psalms reflect lament or complaint. In his book *Spirituality and the Psalms*, Walter Brueggemann identifies the following elements of lament:

- an address to God
- a complaint that is taken to God
- a petition or request for God to act
- a motivation to reinforce the petition
- an anguished request to punish the enemy, and
- an expression of confidence, well-being and gratitude in being heard.

For people of faith who are grieving, laments are a reminder that grief is a part of life.

3. Lament and Grief Reactions:
   10 minutes

One purpose of this study is to highlight how the psalms of lament reflect and express grief. Use the information and additional resources listed in this chapter to introduce common reactions to grief, including those that are:

- physical and behavioral
- emotional
- cognitive
- spiritual, and
- social.

EXTENDED VERSION:
PSALMS AND LAMENT EDUCATIONAL SESSION

If you would like to create an extended session lasting longer than an hour or send participants home with some thought-provoking homework, consider adding the following exercise.

Think of your own life circumstances, the sources of disquiet, distress or despair. Complete the following sentence stems:

I am troubled by...

It has been painful for me to express...

When I try to avoid... I...

I lament...

When I consider the suffering of...

In my silence, I cry for...

I want God to know...

If only God would...

If I could only show or remind God... then God would... then I would be grateful to God at last for...

Reread what you have written. Now take time to write your own psalm of lament to God.

If you have 30 minutes for this exercise in a group setting, allow 15 to 20 minutes for participants to respond to the sentence stems. Then ask people to share some of their responses. Urge them to use these stems as prompts to write their own personal lament at home.

If you have 60 minutes for this exercise in a group setting, use the last 30 minutes for participants to write their own psalms and for some of them to share their poems.

SOURCE: *WRITING THE SACRED: A PSALM-INSPIRED PATH TO APPRECIATING AND WRITING SACRED POETRY*, BY RAY MCGINNIS; NORTHSTONE PUBLISHING, 2005

4. A Psalm of Lament: Small Group Study: 10 minutes

Ask participants to work in pairs or small groups to identify and discuss their reactions to grief expressed by the psalmist. Have participants focus on Psalm 77, verses 1-10. Ask them to identify all of the physical, behavioral, emotional, cognitive, spiritual and social reactions to grief they see in the psalm. You might provide a worksheet with each of these categories and room for participants to fill in the grief reactions they see.

5. Debrief on Insights: 10 minutes

In the large group, debrief about participants' findings to ensure a full picture of signs of grief in the psalm. Ask participants if the psalmist's experience resonates in any way with their own grief experiences.

6. Identify Signs of Confidence and Hope: 10 minutes

Focusing on verses 11–20, ask participants to identify ways the psalmist finds faith and hope. Have participants discuss whether the psalmist's expressions of confidence and hope also resonate with their own grief experiences.

7. Closing: 5 minutes

Close with a reminder that grief is a dynamic process that takes months or years and that all the reactions expressed by the psalmists are possible. At times, people living with grief may connect more with the first ten verses of the psalm. At other times, people may be ready to express confidence and hope. This comes through the grief process itself—not all at once, but over time. Additionally, remind participants that psalms like these help us to resonate with other people's struggles even when we find ourselves in a different place.

A Grief Series

See the chapter titled Creating Unbroken Circles of Care for general ideas on providing an educational series in your congregation. This section mentions some possibilities specifically related to grief.

For example, in fashioning a series of sessions on grief, a Christian congregation might plan a Lenten Series leading up to Easter, leading up to All Saint's Day, or at the close of the liturgical year during late October and November. A Jewish congregation may plan a grief series in connection with the Jewish holidays when Yizkor, a memorial service for the community of bereaved, is recited following the reading of the Torah.

As with the educational programs above, you can customize a series to fit with your faith community's needs. You can also partner with community partners and experts. One example of a Lenten Series using five of the sessions above could feature:

- We Grieve Because We Love: Exploring the Many Facets of Grief

- The Myths and Realities of Grief

- How Grief Works: The Purpose and Dynamics of Grief

- The Spiritual Journey of Grief, and

- The Psalms and Lament.

> *The friend who can be silent with us in a moment of despair or confusion, who can stay with us in an hour of grief and bereavement, who can tolerate not-knowing, not-curing, not-healing and face with us the reality of our powerlessness – that is a friend who cares.*
>
> Henri Nouwen,
> *Out of Solitude*

Additional Resource for Educational Sessions

An additional resource available free online is "The Complete Life Course." Created by Kokua Mau, the end-of-life care coalition in Hawaii, this interactive curriculum was originally designed for faith communities. Many of the one-hour sessions are dedicated to bereavement. Each session has information and exercises that relate to spiritual, cultural, physical and practical aspects of care. Grief topics include: The Journey of Grief, When Grief Becomes Complicated and Cultural and Religious Issues in Mourning.

This resource was developed for use in Hawaii, incorporating cultural and spiritual traditions specific to the islands. Some faith communities may decide to adapt the information for their own use. A coursebook for the series is available online at www.kokuamau.org.

For additional help in planning grief education, see the resources listed in this section of the toolkit, particularly the clergy educational series on page 102.

Congregational Care

Congregations typically mobilize grief support for survivors immediately following death, often extending that support during the days or weeks that follow. However, beyond the first month or two, support is often provided more on an ad hoc basis, if at all. As a result, many people become separated from their congregations during their most intense periods of grieving. They may feel that the congregation has left them behind.

Because grief affects many people and often has lasting and unantici-pated consequences, congregations should ideally organize grief support ministries to help members through the full arc of the grief experience.

See the chapter titled Creating Unbroken Circles of Care for guidance as you begin planning, possibly with your congregational care or health ministries team. The following sections will guide you through strategies, tools and program ideas you can use to create grief support ministries beginning immediately following death and extending after that.

Support Immediately Following Death

Following a death, most bereaved people experience some level of shock. At the same time, they are often required to make funeral arrangements, notify others of the death, write an obituary, make travel arrangements, host out-of-town visitors and deal with other important matters. While some people find it therapeutic to handle these tasks, others are simply overwhelmed by them. Congregations can play an important role for members who need help in dealing with important tasks related to a death.

Clergy Support

If a clergy person was not present when the death occurred, it is crucial to have pastoral contact and presence as soon as possible. For many people, the clergy bring a reminder of God's presence and the support of the faith community. The most significant thing that clergy can do at this point is to listen to the bereaved.

It can be a powerful and sacred conversation for grieving people to describe what it was like for them at the time of the death—especially if they were present. At this point, what matters most for them is the opportunity to tell their story. By listening, you will help facilitate the grieving process. You will also begin to understand the unique nature of the loss and what will be required to customize a plan for grief support.

Often, initial visits with clergy include discussing a funeral or memorial service. The most effective funerals and memorials help people who are grieving remember the person who died. Whether the clergy knew the person well or not at all, it is important to hear the bereaved tell what they remember. One way to accomplish this is by using QUESTIONS FOR REMEMBERING, included below.

QUESTIONS FOR REMEMBERING

In planning funerals or memorial services, it is important for clergy to facilitate conversations with family and friends to learn how they are remembering the one who has died. Here are some sample questions you can ask when talking with individuals or in facilitating a gathered group.

1. When you think of (INSERT NAME) what words best describe his or her personality for you? (Note that saying the name of the person who died helps people with the grieving process and encourages them to use the name themselves.)

2. Which of those words stand out the most for you?

3. Do you have stories or memories that remind you of those aspects of his or her personality?

4. How do you hope people will remember him or her?

5. Were there scriptures or readings that he or she found particularly significant?

6. Did he or she have favorite hymns or music?

7. What was it about those scriptures, readings or music that he or she really loved?

The responses to the first four questions will help you learn more about the one who has died and the nature of the relationship the grieving person had with him or her. These responses will also help you plan a sermon, eulogy or time of remembrance.

The last three questions will help you better understand whether the person had a preferred worship style and may provide specific scripture, readings or music for service planning.

Additional Resources on Clergy Support

Clergy to Clergy: This series was developed by the Hospice Foundation of America to support clergy in their ministry. Topics that relate to grief are: Complicated Mourning, Coping with Loss, Counseling the Bereaved, Facing Grief as a Family and When a Child Dies. Available from the Hospice Foundation of America at www.hospicefoundation.org.

The Clergy End of Life Education Project: Created through a collaboration between the state of Florida and the Hospice Foundation of America, this six-part series is available online in pdf form as a resource for clergy and lay leaders to learn more about congregational care during end of life and grief.

Section four, "The Grief Process: Typical Grief Reactions, Complicated Grief, Anticipatory Grief," provides an excellent overview of the dynamics of grief, integrating spiritual issues. Suitable resource for a self-study or for discussion in a study group. Free through The Hospice Foundation of America at www.hospicefoundation.org/professionalEducation/clergyEducation/documents/book.pdf.

The National Living With Grief Teleconference is a live event telecast each year by the Hospice Foundation of America to participating sites around the county. Organizations such as hospices, hospitals and others host viewing of the event locally. A sampling of past teleconference titles in the "Living With Grief" series, available on DVD, includes: After Sudden Loss, Children and Adolescents, Coping With Public Tragedy and Loss in Later Life.

These teleconferences would make an excellent self-study course or group study. Go to www.hospicefoundation.org to order. For information about attending future telecasts of this series, contact your local hospice or hospital. Participating sites are often open to the community.

BOOKS

All Our Losses, All Our Griefs: Resources for Pastoral Care, **by Kenneth R. Mitchell and Herbert Anderson; Westminster John Knox Press, 1983**

Focuses on types of losses, reactions to loss and unnoticed losses as well as pathways for healing. Enriched by vivid illustrations and case histories.

Complicated Losses, Difficult Deaths: A Practical Guide for Ministering to Grievers, **by Roslyn A. Karaban; Resource Publications, 1999**

Helpful text for clergy and lay leader education or as a source for planning adult education sessions. Includes cases of complicated losses and offers study questions and training exercises.

Grief, Transition and Loss: A Pastor's Practical Guide, **by Wayne Edward Oates; Augsburg Fortress Press Publishers, 1997**

A theological exploration of grief and loss that focuses on the pastor's role.

The Undertaking: Life Studies From the Dismal Trade, **by Thomas Lynch; W.W. Norton & Company, 1998**

Chronicles of small-town life and death told through the unique perspective of undertaker and poet Thomas Lynch, advisor to the TV series "Six Feet Under."

Christian perspectives:

A Grief Observed, **by C.S. Lewis; HarperOne, 2001**

Lament for a Son, **by Nicholas Wolterstorff; Eerdman's Publishing Company, 1987**

Surviving the Death of a Child, **by John Munday with Frances Wohlenhaus-Munday; Westminster John Knox Press, 1995**

Jewish perspectives:

Kaddish, **by Leon Wieseltier; Vintage, 2000**

Living a Year of Kaddish: **A Memoir, by Ari Goldman; Schocken, 2006**

Congregational Support

In addition to helping with funeral or memorial planning, faith communities can offer practical support immediately following the death that can make a real difference. It is important to organize this support so that members offering it are not overwhelmed. One way to do this is for a clergy or lay leader to meet with grieving individuals to determine which things they most want to do themselves and which ones they would like congregation members to do. (See the CONGREGATIONAL GRIEF SUPPORT WISH LIST, page 103.) The person using the list can then help organize congregational support.

Grieving individuals or family members need to know the type of support being provided, when it will occur and the names of the people who will help. If there are too many people involved to name, the individual or family members need to know the name of the person coordinating the group. Because it's often hard for people to remember when they are going through grief, it's helpful for the leader to make a clear list or daily calendar with activities, names and contact information and share that with the individual or family.

In addition to organizing practical support, congregation members can play an important role in offering emotional and spiritual support. As noted for clergy, the most effective support they can offer is by listening. (For additional tips on offering emotional and spiritual support, QUESTIONS FOR REMEMBERING, page 101.)

CONGREGATIONAL GRIEF SUPPORT WISH LIST

Check the tasks below with which the family would like to have help. Your congregation may not be able to do everything, but we want to support you in the most helpful ways possible.

BEFORE AND DURING THE FUNERAL OR MEMORIAL SERVICE:

- Going with one or more family members to a funeral home to make final arrangements.

- Assisting at home by answering the phone, helping with errands or light housekeeping.

- Ensuring that there are staple foods on hand such as bread and milk.

- Recording gifts of food and flowers; this list will help the later on with acknowledgments.

- Arranging for transportation for family members, including airport transportation.

- Hosting guests from out of town.

- Assisting with children.

- Assisting with pets.

- Providing a light breakfast or lunch prior to the memorial service.

- Arranging for someone to stay in the home during visitation and the funeral or memorial service to ensure the safety of the house.

- Coordinating an after-service meal for family and friends.

IMMEDIATELY FOLLOWING THE FUNERAL OR MEMORIAL SERVICE:

- Helping with clean-up at the home.

- Transporting out-of-town guests to the airport.

- Calling to check in during the next few days and weeks.

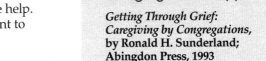

- Help with thank you cards.

- Help returning dishes and other items.

- Offering to bring dinner to drop off or to share.

- Offering to transport the grieving person to worship.

- Helping with light housekeeping or yard work.

- Assisting with children.

- Assisting with pets.

- Helping with paperwork and required filings.

Additional Resources on Congregational Support

Getting Through Grief: Caregiving by Congregations, by Ronald H. Sunderland; Abingdon Press, 1993

A foundation for congregational-based ministry to people who are grieving, emphasizing that congregations need to experience grief education to carry out their mission. Special attention is given to work with children and teenagers and the importance of ongoing grief support groups.

Grief Ministry: Helping Others Mourn, by Donna Reilly Williams and JoAnn Sturzl; Resource Publications, 1992

Explanation of what people do and need when they are experiencing the death of a loved one. A good tool to prepare those who wish to serve on a bereavement team.

Living With Grief: At Work, At School, At Worship, edited by Joyce D. Davidson and Kenneth J. Doka; Routledge, 1999

Aimed mainly at those who work in hospices, but a reminder to anyone working with bereaved people that grief is not confined to the home. Emphasizes the need for plans to be made before a death occurs in the workplace or school.

Living With Grief: Who We Are, How We Grieve, edited by Kenneth J. Doka and Joyce D. Davidson; Routledge, 1998

Emphasizes that one of the prime issues in grief is finding or meaning after the loss, which frequently requires an individual to grapple with a personal belief system and redefine the meaning of spirituality.

Extended Support

Congregational grief support often tapers off in the weeks that follow a death. However, the thoughts, feelings, spiritual questions, physical symptoms and behaviors associated with grief can become more pronounced in the months and years that follow. While some types of practical assistance may still be important, there is often the greatest need for emotional and social support.

Grief Support Packets

One effective strategy some congregations use to communicate the intention to provide ongoing grief support is for a clergy or lay leader to visit within two weeks of the funeral or memorial service to deliver a grief support packet from the faith community.

This packet may include:

- a letter from the clergy that offers support and briefly introduces how the congregation responds during times of grief

- materials such as "There is No Right or Wrong Way to Grieve After a Loss" from Caring Connections (www.caringinfo. org/resources) or another publication that normalizes the grief process

- materials that include potential spiritual questions and concerns people may experience

- information about the congregation's grief support ministries, and

- additional resources for grief support.

Following the visit, plan to offer emotional and social support for at least one year. This may include a combination of cards and letters,

calls, visits and companionship activities offered by individuals, grief support teams and grief support groups. (See the sections below for more detailed guidance on this.) While your congregation may choose not to offer all of these ministries, it is optimal to offer several of them consistently.

These congregational support ministries may be coordinated by an existing congregational care committee or by a grief support leadership group organized specifically for this purpose. While clergy may play a key role in initiating grief support ministries, lay leaders and members can also take the lead in organizing them.

In coordinating grief ministries, it is important to decide whom you will support. While you may choose to focus on "primary grievers" such as spouses or partners, adult children and siblings, you may also decide to offer additional support to other grievers such as grandchildren and close friends.

It is also important to establish a tracking system or calendar to ensure that ministries are offered consistently. A simple spreadsheet or card file system can help a grief leadership team track the support provided, such as a monthly check-in call, a quarterly visit and cards and letters on anniversaries and other special days.

Cards and Letters

Although faith communities report that cards and letters are the primary way they offer grief support, even the simple task of sending meaningful messages c an feel overwhelming when you are looking for the appropriate words to offer.

Tips for Writing Effective Condolence Notes

When writing a condolence note or letter, consider the tips offered below.

Always write a note. Receiving many notes around the time of a death is a powerful experience. Even if you've waited a while, write the note.

Make it simple. Even a short note can be effective when written with empathy.

Use a conversational tone. Instead of writing formally, consider your note to be your half of a genuine conversation with the person who is grieving.

Avoid clichés. Reflect your thoughts as directly and authentically as you can. Some clichés, in fact, may be more harmful than helpful, such as "Don't cry; he's in a better place," "God needed another angel in heaven" or "It was all just a part of God's plan."

Remember that each loss is unique. Even if you have experienced a similar death, don't assume that the grieving person's experience is the same as yours.

Focus on the grieving person. As you write your note, keep your primary focus on the other person. If you choose to share your own experience, do so with the intention of offering empathy and support. For example, instead of saying: "You have to take break." consider saying: "One thing that really helped me was..." Keep your personal sharing short and to the point.

Consider using the form sketched out below.

- Acknowledge the death. By acknowledging that the person has died, you help the grieving people with the task of coming to terms with the reality of their loss.

- Express your care and concern. Never assume you know what the grieving person is thinking or feeling.

- Include an anecdote, story or remembrance. People particularly appreciate knowing how you remember the person who died, some way in which he or she touched your life or stays in your memory. It helps them with the task of remembering and may spur them to share their stories with you, which can be a therapeutic way for them to work through their grief.

- Use a closing that is meaningful for you. Remind the recipient of your continuing care or your wish as he or she goes through grief.

While email often eclipses sending traditional letters, do not underestimate the power of a handwritten remembrance. Cards and letters are recommended following the death, on special days such as birthdays, holidays and other events. Cards that recognize the anniversary of a person's death are also a meaningful support.

One way to encourage this activity is for congregations to help members feel more comfortable writing notes. A newsletter article on writing condolence notes can be effective. This article could incorporate the author's personal insights from writing notes with the tips outlined above. Ideally, the article would include a quote or story from a member who appreciated this personalized form of support.

Another strategy to help members become more comfortable with writing these notes is to offer a workshop on writing the condolence notes. This could include giving participants the opportunity to share their experiences receiving helpful and unhelpful card and letters, tips on writing the note and an exercise writing a note they have been delaying or wish they had written.

Grief Notes: The Power of Pen and Paper

Mike Queen has been the senior pastor of First Baptist Church, Wilmington, North Carolina—a large, multi-staff congregation—for 22 years. When he began his pastorate, he asked for a list of congregational members who had immediate family members die in the past year: a spouse, a parent, a son or daughter. He was given a list of about 10 people.

Using this list as a starting place, Queen began a ministry of pastoral grief support letters. He has a simple system of recording the names and dates of death on a 3 X 5 card. Then he identifies the relatives who will receive his note and adds their names to the card. He keeps the cards in order by date and checks for the upcoming anniversaries of deaths regularly.

Two or three days before the anniversary of the person's death, he sends a handwritten note letting the relatives know that he is thinking of them and praying for them as they remember the person who died. Queen sends an anniversary note every year for five years following the death. When he reaches the fifth year, he lets the member know that that this will be his final note but that he will pray for this person on this day every year. Then he moves this 3 X 5 card to a separate stack for prayer only.

Queen now prays and sends notes to hundreds of members a year who are living with loss, prompted by a stack of cards that has grown more than four inches thick.

Over the years, members have expressed how much this ministry means to them in many ways. One day, Queen was visiting a member whose husband had died some years before. While he was there, she went to a drawer and pulled out all five years of notes he had written to her, notes she had treasured.

Recently, Queen came to the card of the first person he buried more than 20 years before. He prayed for the man's wife that morning and went about his day. On the way home, he stopped for gas. As he stood at the pump, he looked across and saw the woman he had prayed for that morning. He went over to her, put his arm around her and said: "I thought of you this morning and kept you in my prayers." She said: "I know you did. You are the only one who remembers."

When Queen's father died, a member of the congregation came up to him and said: "Next year you will receive a card from me."

Calls and Visits

Calls and visits in the months following a death can make a significant contribution to a person's grieving process. Just as with all supportive calls and visits, it is important to:

- listen with empathy and understanding

- gently explore people's thoughts, feelings, experiences and beliefs in an open, supportive way

- refrain from judgment and attempts to comfort that cover up or short-circuit strong feelings and thoughts

- proceed at the same pace emotionally that the person is going

- be willing to engage the spiritual questions, and

- offer a supportive presence.

Some specific reminders for calls and visits are included here.

Make it personal. Find natural ways to talk about the person who died, using his or her name—and also mentioning specific ways you are keeping his or her memory alive.

Encourage storytelling. Honor the importance that grieving people place on telling stories; it allows them to help process the grief. Some people will need to share certain stories numerous times. Listen to what they are saying and support them in discovering meaning.

Acknowledge grief as "normal." Respect each person's unique experience of grief. At the same time, find ways to normalize it so that they know that what they are experiencing is part of the grieving process.

Note changes. As you call and visit over time, listen for changes. Be especially attuned to the tasks of grieving and where people are in relation to them. This will help guide your support. Make referrals to grief support professionals if the person does not seem to be making progress.

Heed the meaningful dates. Be sensitive to monthly and annual anniversaries of the death, as well as birthdays and other special days. Ask how you can be supportive during the holidays and other special days.

Spiritual Support

As discussed above, grief inevitably raises spiritual questions and concerns, which in turn raises the need for specialized sensitivity, education and support.

Individual Support

Effective spiritual support through grief that honors a person's questions and suffering helps him or her come to a new and often deeper experience of faith while working through the process.

In offering care and support for the spiritual effects of grief, bear in mind the points highlighted below.

Take spiritual questions seriously. Reassure people that doubts and questions are part of the process and normal for all people—including people of faith.

Acknowledge the suffering. Support people in their pain as they explore the spiritual questions. Reaffirm God's presence in the midst of suffering.

Affirm insights. Members may also express spiritual strengths that have emerged for them during their grief. For example, people may say:

- I feel God has been with me though this difficult time.

- My faith in God has kept me going.

- Reading scripture and praying comforts me.

Affirm these insights as a way to help strengthen their faith.

(See Incorporating Grief Into Worship, beginning on page 115, for more on spiritual support.)

Companionship

Offering companionship for the grieving person can be a ministry in and of itself. The mere act of spending time with the person reaffirms your relationship and his or her connection to the community.

However, beware that social withdrawal is a normal part of the grieving process. Be prepared for people to turn down invitations. When this happens, let them know you want to keep in touch—and ask if you can call again.

Members can offer companionship to grieving people by:

- offering to bring a meal and eat together or to go out for coffee or a meal

- going on outings to a place the person enjoys, such as a park, favorite shop or a concert

- going with a person to worship to help ease the transition, and

- accompanying the person to the cemetery.

Grief Support Teams

Some faith communities form grief support teams to help coordinate effective grief support over time. Grief teams are generally composed of four to 12 team members who learn the team approach. Working together, they offer practical, emotional, spiritual and social support for people living with grief. To get the best fit for their talents and time, ask them what they enjoy doing most and when they are available.

In putting together a plan, put yourself in the position of the individual or family. It is important to tailor a plan for each person that fits his or her individual grief. Some people desire more interaction and support; some desire less. Think about what signs of support people receive from the congregation month by month—and be prepared to offer some type of help for as long as two years after a death occurs.

By involving a number of volunteers, no individual becomes overwhelmed trying to do it all. And appointing one or more leaders helps ensure that the efforts are coordinated rather than duplicated or incomplete.

Teaming Up to Provide Help Away From Home

Tracey was a college sophomore when she received word that her sister had disappeared without a trace in a large metropolitan city. Tracey suddenly became concerned about her own personal security miles away from any source of family comfort and support. To complicate things Tracey was still grieving the loss of her father, who had died suddenly just one year earlier.

Tracey's friends in her faith community quickly realized they needed to step up and do what friends do naturally—love and support each other. Six of Tracey's closest friends met early one Saturday morning and developed a plan for supporting their friend through this unimaginable grief.

They began by responding to her immediate needs. They created a schedule with friends taking turns being with Tracey constantly during the first two weeks to help her get through the day. Team members also coordinated meals, ran errands, made calls. Because they coordinated their efforts, no individual was overwhelmed.

Following the initial weeks, Tracey's friends met again to learn more formally about the support team model and how they could sustain their support for Tracey during the months ahead. Tracey's biggest need was for companionship: people who would do check in on her, spend time with her, go places with her. Coordinating with Tracey, the team met monthly to plan six weeks of companionship in advance so that Tracey would have a calendar of support.

The team used some of their monthly meeting time to learn more about the unique nature of traumatic loss and how to offer support. They also shared with each other about their own experience supporting Tracey. This coordinated support helped reassure Tracey that she was not alone at this most difficult time and gave the congregation a clear and organized way to offer care and support.

Additional Resource on Grief Support Teams

Project Compassion, **www.project-compassion.org** **or 919-402-1844**

This nonprofit organization in Chapel Hill, North Carolina, partners with the National Support Team Network to provide resources, coaching and training on the team approach to community-based care.

Grief Support Groups

Grief support groups give people the opportunity to share their experiences of grief and loss in a safe, supported setting. In addition, effective groups often help participants develop a fuller understanding of the grief process and gain the skills they need to cope with grief and loss.

Local hospice, hospital or nonprofit organizations may already operate such support groups. However, offering one through your faith community ensures that your members will have an accessible, safe space for sharing their grief experiences with other members. The following outline offers one model for conducting a time-limited group. (See the additional resources listed on page 109 for more grief group formats.)

No one ever told me that grief felt so like fear.

Author C.S. Lewis

The model for a faith community support group described here is for four weeks, 1½ hours per session. While the fourth session incorporates concepts that are specific to the Christian faith, that portion can be adapted for other faith traditions.

Session 1

- Begin with a devotional reading from Exodus 19:4. This passage portrays God as the mother eagle who will not let us fall.

- Introduce the purpose of the group and discuss the support group guidelines. (See below.)

- Ask members of the group to introduce themselves and to share the story of why they are there.

- Introduce the topic of grief. Make certain you include grief as a healthy process and active choice; also cover the purpose and tasks of grief. (For background information, see pages 90 through 96.)

- As a homework assignment, ask grief group members to explore what it is like to feel grief. Request that members keep a journal about their grief experiences and the feelings that accompany them. Ask them to bring pictures of their loved ones to share with the group and help them tell their story.

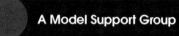

Session 2

- Begin with a devotional reading from Isaiah 49:13-16a. This reading reminds us that God will not always protect us from pain, harm or suffering but will always be with us.

- Discuss last week's homework. Invite participants to share pictures of loved ones with the group and to discuss memories that arise.

- Introduce the grief task of adjusting to life after loss.

- For homework, ask each member to make a concrete change in his or her life—no matter how small. This will encourage everyone to take an action toward change.

Session 3

- Begin with a reading from Isaiah 40:28-31. This passage speaks to God's faithfulness and empowering grace.

- Share the homework responses.

- Introduce depression and talk about symptoms. (See *Counseling Depressed Women*, by Susan J. Dunlap; Westminster Press, 1997 or another pastoral counseling resource to learn more about depression.) Ask a community professional to facilitate this part if needed. Affirm each participant's courageous choice to grieve.

- Ask members to divide into small groups of about three, depending on the size of the whole. Invite groups to share where they are in their grief and then pray for each other.

- Introduce the grief task of emotionally relocating one who has died: "learning to love the person who died in a new way" or "learning to love them in their absence rather than their presence."

- For homework, ask members to either write a prayer of commendation to God that gives thanks for the person who has died, explicitly putting him or her in God's hands, or to write a letter to the deceased.

- End with a prayer or a hymn.

Session 4

- Begin with a reading from 1 Thessalonians 4:13. This reading reminds participants that they do not have to grieve as those who have no hope, but must learn how to live as fully as possible without a loved one, recognizing that we can learn how to love him or her in another way.

- Ask people to write a response to the question: What are your hopes for your life?

- Invite them to begin writing a plan of action. Encourage realistic hopes.

- (Optional) Move to sanctuary. Remind participants of their own baptism and of what they hope for in faith.

- Read prayers of commendation.

- Close with a prayer or a hymn.

Developed by Susan J. Dunlap, Adjunct Professor, Duke Divinity School

SUPPORT GROUP GUIDELINES

ATTENDANCE

A grief group works best when everyone in the group makes a firm commitment to show up for every session. You are asked to make that commitment. Of course there will be times when you are sick or have other unavoidable commitments. This group is scheduled so that it does not conflict with any other programs associated with the congregation.

ADVICE

We are not here to offer advice. We are here to give direct reports of our own experiences and feelings. If you have had similar feelings or experiences, let someone know what worked for you, rather than saying: "If I were you, I would…"

TEARS

Crying is natural and healthy. While crying outside this room is not always possible or safe, in this group, when you are into deep feelings, when your insides are in pain, when your throat is choked up, give yourself permission to cry freely without embarrassment.

CREATING SPACE FOR GRIEF

In our society, a common response to a grieving person is to give a pat on the back, words of comfort, a tissue for tears or reassurance. While these actions may be well-intentioned, they also have the effect of short-circuiting the grief experience. In this group, we will refrain from these actions to allow others to fully experience their thoughts and feelings. We can often be far more caring by being attentive listeners. The leader will demonstrate that silence can offer space for all feelings to be fully heard without a rush to comfort.

COMFORT

While our intention is not to shut one another down as we experience grief, it is quite appropriate at any time for you to seek comfort from others. Holding up four fingers is our sign for a pat on the back, a kind word, a touch on the arm. Tissues will be available nearby.

TOLERANCE

We are not here to judge each other, but to listen and offer understanding. We sometimes find the experiences, expressions and feelings of others to be completely foreign to our own experience, upbringing or value system. We learn to lovingly accept everything expressed here as totally legitimate for the person expressing it.

CONFIDENTIALITY

The only way we can be comfortable sharing with one another is to be certain that all that is said here will stay here. That means we do not discuss what happens outside of this room with anyone for any reason, even without mentioning names. We just don't.

Additional Resources on Grief Support Groups

The Art of Grief: The Use of Expressive Arts in a Grief Support Group, J. Earl Rogers; Routledge, 2007

Includes an eight-session curriculum integrating arts for use with grief support groups.

Bereavement Ministry: A Leader's Resource Manual, by Harriet Young with the Diocese of Rapid City; Twenty-Third Publications, 1997

A Catholic resource manual offers detailed directions for organizing or improving grief support groups in dioceses, parishes, college campuses and many other community situations. Includes handouts and reflection questions for each session.

The Bereavement Ministry Program: A Comprehensive Guide for Churches, by Jan Nelson and David Aaker; Ave Maria Press, 1998

Guidebook teaching clergy and lay ministers to minister to those who are working their way through the grieving process. Includes basic resources for adults, children and teenagers, along with a comprehensive guide to setting up a bereavement support group and a CD containing resources.

The Florida Hospital Pastoral Care Department: www.floridahospital.com

Offers online resources for grief support, including practical tips for one-on-one grief support and a step-by-step guide to starting your own bereavement ministry.

The Understanding Your Grief Support Group Guide, by Alan Wolfelt; 2004

Available at www.centerforloss.com, a website dedicated to providing articles, books, and other resources to for grieving individuals and families.

Grief Support Quilters

As discussed in Creating Unbroken Circles of Care (pages 9 and 33), some faith communities and hospices are integrating various arts into grief support groups. For example, Angela Hospice in Livinoa, Michigan formed The Grief Support Quilters. Group members meet twice a month for two hours. Using clothing that their loved ones have worn, they create quilts and pillows for their own use and for family members. Members share thoughts, feelings and remembrances informally as they quilt. Sewing skill is not required. Instructors help participants with the "how tos" to realize their visions.

According to the social worker who facilitates the group, it is "the perfect group for individuals who don't feel comfortable in a traditional group format."

For more information, go to www.angelahospice.org.

Support for Grieving Children

Faith communities can make an important difference in the lives of children by supporting them in their grief and by teaching their parents how to care for them as they experience it. Begin by learning about how grief affects children as they develop. (See Children, Teens and Grief, page 95.)

A number of tangible tips for dealing with grieving children are also offered here.

- Use language they understand. Simple concrete language that reflects what children can see, hear, feel and touch communicates well. When talking about death, use words such as "died" rather than "passed away" or "gone on a long trip." This will help keep children from imagining that the person is coming back.

- Answer their questions. When children ask difficult questions, they are signaling a desire to learn. Assure them that it is good for them to ask questions. Respond to them as directly and truthfully as possible.

- Ask them to repeat what you told them. Confirm that the child understands what you are saying and clarify as needed.

- Listen for thoughts, feelings and other grief reactions. While the youngest children will express grief through behavior, as children become able to talk about their thoughts and feelings, they will express them. Instead of telling children that you know how they feel, listen to what they said and follow up with a question, such as "How does that make you feel?" or "What do you think about that?"

- Share your own feelings. As an adult, you can model talking about your feelings with children. Talking about love is particularly significant during times of grief and loss.

- Talk about the person who died. Encourage children to share memories. Use the name of the person who died. This gives children added permission to talk about the person.

- Remember that each child will grieve differently. Respect differing grief styles and make sure each child receives the kind of encouragement and support needed.

- Offer choices. When it comes to funerals, for example, help children understand that they are a way to say goodbye to the person who died. Help them understand what will happen and give them the choice to attend, but do not force them to go. Children may want to help with some of the preparations. Or they may participate in some way in the service by sharing something they have written, drawn or remembered.

- Help them remember. Having special items from the person who died may also help a child remember him or her. For example, if a grandfather and grandson used to go fishing together, the grand-

Additional Resources on Helping Grieving Children

Caring Connections: www.caringinfo.org

Offers Helping Children Cope With the Death of a Loved One, a resource with tips and additional information on supporting children and grief.

The Dougy Center: www.dougy.org

Provides resources for children, teens and parents with links to local programs.

Partnership for Parents: www.partnershipforparents.org

Contains a section articles on grief for parents of children who have died.

BOOKS

Children & Grief: When a Parent Dies, by J. William Worden; Guilford Press, 1996

Drawing upon extensive interviews and assessments of children who have lost a parent to death, this book offers a portrait of the mourning process in children.

Children Mourning: Mourning Children, edited by Kenneth J. Doka; Routledge Publishing, 1995

Explores three basic themes in children's grief: that their understanding of death and their reactions to illness and loss constantly change, that they grieve in ways both different from and similar to adults and that they need significant support as they grieve.

son may value having his grand-father's fishing rod.

- Respect the way children grieve. Children may talk seriously about grief one moment and turn around and play the next moment as if nothing had happened. Playing and having fun are important for children. It helps them cope with the grief process. For example, following the funeral of a beloved grandmother, some young cousins organized a homespun carnival in the backyard with games and prizes because their grandmother loved to have fun. Now adults, these cousins still remember that carnival many years later.

In supporting families following death, remember that faith community members may have the opportunity to talk with children at various times during their grief journeys. Remember also that your congregation may help parents learn how to support their children through grief. By caring for children's grief, your faith community will help them cope more effectively with grief throughout their lives.

Support for Grieving Teens

When teenagers experience grief, they respond to support that fits with their personalities, grief styles, growth and development. While they may talk with parents and other family members, teens are most likely to turn to friends and people outside their family for support. Faith communities may have key opportunities to offer them support.

Here are some pointers to keep in mind when helping teens who are experiencing grief.

- Teens are full-fledged grievers. It is important to understand that they experience the full range of physical, emotional, cognitive, spiritual and social impacts of grief.

- Grief may create fear or anxiety. Because the emotions surrounding grief are often strong, they might seem overwhelming for some teens. It is helpful to reassure teens that grief is normal and natural. Encourage them to talk about their thoughts and feelings.

- Teens tend to reject labels. Being told that they are experiencing a certain stage of grief or the "right and wrong ways" to grieve will cause most teens to back away. Listen to each individual's unique grief experience and learn from it rather than attempting to instruct him or her about grief.

- Teens may attempt to hide their true feelings. They may receive cues from parents and others that their grief feelings are not acceptable and choose to keep them to themselves. Encourage teens to express themselves openly.

- Teens may feel isolated. Their friends may not understand what they are experiencing, causing them to feel alone. Also, if the person for whom they are grieving died traumatically, they may experience stigma from others or reluctance to talk about their feelings. Having safe individuals with whom they can talk can make a difference. Talking with other teens the same age who have experienced loss may help.

- Teens may regress or act out. Just as grieving adults may engage in risky behavior such as violence, sex, alcohol or drug abuse, teens may also use high-risk behavior to avoid the pain of grief. Help them deal with the pain of the loss and offer them constructive activities and ways to remember the person who died, such as creating a garden, writing in a journal, putting together a memorial basketball game.

- Teen grief will last for a long time. While grief will shift and change as the teenager grieves, it will go on. Be patient in offering support and connecting them with healthy ways to grieve.

One way to support teens in your congregation is to offer a teen grief support groups. There is a free model for creating a teen group at www.hospicenorthcoast.org/pdf/teengriefgroups.pdf. This teen grief curriculum is a compilation of activities and handouts that includes an introductory section on setting up and running a group followed by an eight-week curriculum.

If your congregation is unable to offer a teen grief support group on your own, consider joining with other congregations, or refer teens to an existing community-based program. If no services are available, link them with online support.

Additional Resources on Helping Grieving Teens

The Grieving Teen: A Guide for Teenagers and Their Friends, by Helen Fitzgerald; Fireside Publishing, 2000

Addresses the special needs of adolescents struggling with loss and gives them the tools to work through their pain and deal with concerns including family changes, issues with friends and problems at school.

Straight Talk About Death for Teens: How to Cope With Losing Someone You Love, by Earl Grollman; Beacon Press, 1993

Offers advice and answers the questions that teens are likely to ask themselves when grieving the death of someone close.

Support Following Traumatic Death

While every grief experience is unique and significant, grief that follows a trauma such as accident, disaster, murder, suicide or death of a child may seem especially overwhelming. Grief after traumatic death may create powerful emotions, including intense fear and rage. It may bring unexpected and possibly violent thoughts of destruction or revenge. For many people, spiritual beliefs and relationships may be rocked to the core. Family members may be radically affected. People often do not "get over" traumatic death; it changes them for life.

Few situations challenge congregations more than knowing how to care for people who are traumatized. This section discusses the particular grief that people experience following trauma and suggests ways that congregation leaders and members can respond.

In addition to the information here, learning more about Post Traumatic Stress Disorder (PTSD) will help you understand the types of challenges people face and how to approach them. (To learn more about PTSD, go to the National Institute of Mental Health: www.nimh.nih.gov/health/topics/post-traumatic-stress-disorder-ptsd/index.shtml.) With all grief following traumatic death, watch for signs of traumatic grief and help connect people with professional counselors who specialize in traumatic grief when possible.

Accidental Death or Disaster

To prepare yourself for supporting people following accident or disaster, begin by gaining a full understanding of the basic grief process described in this chapter. By becoming more comfortable supporting people through grief in general, you prepare yourself to provide care and support when death is unexpected.

In addition, it is important to understand factors specific to sudden, unexpected loss. News of death by accident or disaster can radically alter the course of a survivor's life.

Shock often plays a major role at first in protecting people from the full reality of the loss. Survivors often do not believe that the person has died. They may feel lost and confused, unable to concentrate and make decisions. They may be unable to make arrangements and plans or care for themselves in the short term. It can take some time for people to begin to accept the reality of the death. This is particularly complicated when there is no body, such as following a plane crash or other disaster.

As the shock wears off and the reality of the loss begins to sink in, the impact of grief can be intense. With no time to say goodbye before a death, people may have a profound sense of unfinished business. They may blame God, the person who caused the accident or disaster or even the person who died. They may experience unexpected rage or helplessness. They may wonder how their loved one felt when dying. And they may be traumatized not only by the death but also by the way they learned about the death. All of these factors become part of the grief experience.

Tips for Support After Accidental Death or Disaster

As you support people following sudden loss, keep the following in mind.

Survivors often lose a sense of order and control. A loss of control is often especially acute soon after the death occurs. Helping people with daily routines can assist them in regaining some grounding.

Survivors lose a sense of security and safety. Help reassure people that they are safe when that is true.

Empathy makes a difference. Let them know that you are sorry, that you cannot know what they are feeling but that you care.

Survivors often have no point of reference. Let them know that their reactions such as anger or feeling like they are going crazy are normal reactions; it's the situation that is not normal.

Let them know you care about them spiritually. Reassure them that you will be praying for them and that you will keep in contact with them if you are able to do so.

For many people, sudden death raises spiritual questions in an acute way. They may ask:

- Why did God let this happen?

- Why did he or she die this way?

- Couldn't God have prevented it?

- Why did that person die and not me?

- What could I have done to change this?

All of these questions are valid expressions of grief. When a person's faith and faith community helps respond to these deep questions and grief experiences, faith becomes an asset. When it fails to respond or is not helpful in responding, it can become part of the trauma itself.

Additional Resources on Sudden Loss

Congregational Trauma: Caring, Coping, and Learning, by Jill M. Hudson; Alban Institute, 1998

Argues that forgiveness is a true theological concept that allows people to cope with the pain and grief of loss.

Living With Grief After Sudden Loss, edited by Kenneth J. Doka; Taylor & Francis, 1996

Examines the subject of abrupt, unexpected death and its effects and implications for the survivors. Topics covered include: after heart attack and stroke, survivors of suicide, complicated grief in the military and grief counseling.

Homicide

When death is the result of a violent, forceful act, survivors may experience guilt or anger that they were not able to protect their loved one. They may feel rage toward the person who committed the murder. They may feel loss of control or a fear that they are now potential victims. They may have nightmares about the murder or flashbacks if they witnessed it.

In addition to loss of the individual, survivors of murder deal with law enforcement, the criminal justice system, the media and people around them who may or may not understand what happened.

Tips for Support Following Homicide

As you support people following murder, review the tips for supporting people following accident and disaster on page 112. In addition, there are a number of other points to bear in mind.

Specialized support may be needed. Individuals and families may be involved in legal proceedings for years. Grief support may include helping them find resources, advocacy and support. If the media is involved, you may add media management to the kind of support you offer.

Be nonjudgmental. Survivors may feel stigmatized or judged because of the death. Consistent, nonjudgmental support is especially important in these circumstances.

Remain calm. When supporting people following murder, as with all people who are grieving, cultivate offering a non-anxious presence.

Suicide

Grief that follows suicide is often extremely intense and has a long-lasting impact. Most people have no previous experience with unexpected, violent death. Whatever helped them with loss in the past will probably not help initially after a suicide.

Family members may have witnessed the suicide or found the body and had to interact with police and other officials who responded to the scene. They may have dealt with questioning, claiming the body, cleaning up after the suicide and other traumatic experiences.

One of the primary reactions suicide survivors have is guilt. They often blame themselves for not seeing signs or for not doing something to prevent the situation. It is important to reassure people that the suicide was not their fault.

As family members and others begin to grieve, people frequently search for the reason the person committed suicide. Suicide notes and other communications from the person who died can cause either comfort or distress. When they experience distress, mourners should be encouraged not to take notes literally. Suicide often results from deep depression, a potential lethal illness that can result in death. You may find it helpful to let survivors know that their loved one died as a result of an illness.

People of faith may struggle with how they believe God views suicide, wondering if God finds it "forgivable." In many traditions, it is theologically consistent to reassure survivors that there is nothing that can separate their loved one from God's love.

Support for Grieving People After Suicide

As with all losses, different approaches will work with different people. However, caring support is always important. Here are some tips for providing support to other following a suicide.

Offer your presence. You can offer support just by being there.

Normalize the grief. Help people know that emotional turmoil and conflicting feeling are part of the process.

Listen with empathy. Make room for people to say what they are thinking and feeling. Do not rush them to understand or to sort it out.

Help identify support. Although they may not choose to contact them, help grieving people remember those who might take helpful roles in supporting them best.

Encourage contacting local resources. Most communities, often through hospitals or social service agencies, offer seminars and support groups for those grieving about a suicide. Survivors benefit particularly from the support of other suicide survivors, helping them feel less alone.

Additional Resources on Suicide

Clergy Responses to Suicidal Persons and Their Family Members, by David C. Clark; Exploration Press, 1993

Healing After the Suicide of a Loved One, by Ann Smolin and John Guinan; Simon & Schuster, 1993

No Time to Say Goodbye: Surviving the Suicide of a Loved One, by Carla Fine; Main Street Books, 1999

Death of a Child

Say My Child's Name

*The mention of my child's name
may bring tears to my eyes,
But it never fails
to bring music to my ears.*

*If you are really my friend,
let me hear the music of her name!
It soothes my broken heart
and sings to my soul!*

AUTHOR UNKNOWN

People expect that children will grow and mature in the "natural order" of things. But when a child dies, that cycle is broken. A child's death may bring a loss of innocence, a loss of hopes and dreams, a loss of understanding the world.

While friends and other relatives are often profoundly affected by a child's death, is often said that the grief parents experience is the most intense known. Because of the relationship between parent and child, parents say they feel when a child dies that a part of their being has been ripped away.

The despair that parents experience may include a sense that life is not worth living, that they have failed as parents, that they should have found a way to keep their child from dying or that they should not go on living since their child had died. Parents also may fear working through or "letting go" of their grief because of a fear that will mean letting go of their child.

In addition, parents often describe powerful feelings of disorientation. Parents will always be the parent of the child who has died; this relationship is not taken away by death. However, they will not be able to nurture that child in life, helping him or her to grow and mature. The contradiction of being parent and not being able to parent is often profound.

The death of a child can also have a profound effect on marriages. Mothers and fathers often work through their grief in different ways. Not addressed, different grief experiences and grieving styles can significantly strain or break marital relationships. (See Beyond Grief and Gender: A Matter of Style, page 94, for more on this.) For example, if a father's grieving style focuses on instrumental grieving and he is culturally expected to be "the strong one," a father's grief often becomes overlooked and less supported. In this situation, grief specialists report that mothers often become seen as "primary grievers" and fathers as "second class" or "forgotten grievers."

In supporting all grieving parents, it is important to give them opportunities to fully express their unique grief. It is most important for the intensity, power and duration of their pain to be acknowledged and for their continuing roles as parents to be honored.

One of the most significant tasks grieving parents work though is finding ways to keep the memory of their child alive. As a result, they may experience great difficulty deciding what to do with a child's clothes, belongings or room. It is important to encourage parents to find ways to hold onto and treasure the memories and items that are meaningful for them. Rituals of remembrance can be particularly important for parents and families.

Along with keeping memories and items, grieving parents may puzzle over what to do for birthdays, holidays, Mother's Day, Father's Day and the anniversary of the child's death. They may need to be supported as they make decisions that help them continue the relationship of memory with their child.

As time passes, some parents and families will find strength and hope through your faith community, beliefs and tradition. However, even the most faithful parents may experience spiritual crisis and need additional spiritual support. They may ask question such as "Why did this happen to my child?" "Why did God allow this?" and "Why did God abandon me or my child?" (See Spiritual Support, page 106, for more specifics on this.)

Tips for Supporting Parents After a Child's Death

Because the death of a child changes the life of parent and family members, it's important for congregations to be prepared to offer helpful support. In addition to the guidance throughout this grief chapter, here are some tips on providing support.

Acknowledge the child's death. Tell the parents about your sadness for them, your care and support.

Be present. Avoiding the parents and their grief increases the isolation they may feel.

Talk about the child. Use their child's name as a way to remember. If they are willing to talk, ask to see photos or mementos.

Offer practical and specific support. Offer concrete ways to support them, such as bringing a meal, or doing something special with them, such as running errands or just spending time with them.

Remember special days. Talk with the parents about their thoughts and feelings on days such as the child's birthday or the anniversary of his or her death.

Respect their grief process. Let them set the tone with you and remember that the journey is a long one.

Additional Resources for Grieving Parents

Lament for a Son, by Nicholas Wolterstorff; **William B. Eerdman's Publishing, 1987**

Explores different facets of grief through brief vignettes, from the perspective of a father grieving the loss of his son.

Living With Grief: Children and Adolescents, **edited by Kenneth J. Doka & Amy S. Tucci; Hospice Foundation of America, 2008**

Addresses developmental perspectives, the dying child and supporting children and adolescents through grief and loss.

Parental Loss of a Child, **edited by Therese A. Rando; Research Press, 1986**

Examines a wide range of topics related to parental grief and offers clinical interventions and support procedures for helping bereaved parents.

Incorporating Grief Into Worship

But I, O Lord, cry out to you;
in the morning my prayer
comes before you.
Oh Lord, why do you cast me off?
Why do you hide your face from me?

PSALM 88: 13-14

While some people experiencing grief may find participating in worship a spiritually nurturing experience, others may find it difficult or impossible. In addition to the natural social withdrawal that can occur as part of the grief process, the content of worship itself may not fully include grieving people, so they may find it somewhat alien and unapproachable.

In faith communities, grief is most frequently incorporated into funeral or memorial rituals. However, these services occur near the beginning of the grief process, while the most intense reactions to grief often occur weeks or months after a person's death.

One way to offer more far-sighted support is to create services specifically for people who are grieving. In addition, congregations may offer annual services at special times of the year that honor the grief that all people face.

By integrating an authentic understanding of grief into worship throughout the year, you provide more consistent support for people living with it. You also send a signal that your faith community cares about people as they go through grief and is open to sharing the journey with them.

As described in the chapter titled Creating Unbroken Circles of Care, support for people living with grief can be woven into many aspects of worship—including scripture, readings, sermons, personal stories or testimonies, music, dance and liturgical arts. This section describes some specific ways and times that faith communities can reach out to those experiencing grief.

Funerals and Memorial Services

Of all the areas connected with grief support, funerals and memorial services have received the most attention. Many faith traditions have well defined rituals and services available as resources, but there is often room for clergy to customize them meaningfully for individual situations.

A carefully designed funeral or memorial service that fully honors the person who has died and lays the groundwork for people to

After desolation, grief brings back our humanity.

Aphorist Mason Cooley

experience grief within the faith community can be a significant gift for people in your congregation.

While assessing your congregation's funerals and memorial services, note the critiques people most frequently offer of how these services fall short.

Not personal enough. Relying on tradition and prepared services is not enough. Just as each life and each experience of grief is unique, each service should be uniquely designed for each individual.

Exclusive focus on life after death. Helping people remember the person who has died by recalling unique aspects of his or her life is a key purpose of grieving. Creating opportunities for remembering is a key element of an effective service and can help significantly with that process.

Tips for Planning Funerals and Memorial Services

Here are some tips to remember when planning funerals and memorial services.

Schedule a meeting with the family. Set aside sufficient time, often one and a half to two hours, to help plan the services with involved family members. Ask them what people they think should be involved in this meeting.

Take time to listen. Even if you knew the person who died well, it is important to hear the family's exact words at this time and get their varied points of view. This will help with service preparation and help people who are grieving with the grief process. (See Questions for Remembering, page 101, for specific guidance on this.)

Write down words, memories, stories and legacies. Incorporate these personal memories into the sermon or time for remembering or quoting people who are grieving. This approach will help reflect the life of the person who died more authentically and will give grieving people a voice in the service when it would be difficult for them to speak themselves.

Normalize grief as part of the service. Help people understand that grief can affect people in many ways. Reinforce that the faith community will be there for support.

Don't forget the children. If you anticipate children will attend the service, consider a children's sermon that addresses grief. One pastor who makes this a practice talks very straightforwardly with children about what grief is and about God's presence with them during grief. This can be helpful for the children during the service and can also model later as parents talk with their children.

Honor the spiritual questions. For example, when death is sudden or sudden and unexpected, give voice to the "why" questions as part of the service. Acknowledge your own ignorance as well as affirming what you do know.

Lack of attention to grief. Some services focus so much on hope, a long life or a life well lived that the pain of the loss and the complexity of grief are ignored. Just because a person has lived a long and faithful life does not mean that survivors will not grieve the loss. By fully honoring all losses as part of the service, you create space for grieving people to engage in healthy grief work—and send a message that the congregation is there for them.

Additional Resources on Funeral and Memorial Services

Calvin Institute of Christian Worship: www.calvin.edu/worship/planning/5_09_04.php

Website including worship resources for funerals and memorial services.

Funeral Consumers Alliance: www.funerals.org

Website offering general information about planning funerals and memorial services, along with local resources.

***Funeral Services: Just in Time*, by Cynthia L. Danals; Abingdon Press, 2007**

Offers examples of funeral services for difficult situations—including children and teens and sudden and violent deaths. Each service is set in a ministry context and includes a sample sermon, Scripture text and prayers.

***The Perfect Stranger's Guide to Funerals and Grieving Practices*, by Stuart M. Matlins; Skylight Paths Publishing, 2000**

Introduces the history and belief system of 38 different denominations and religions and then details appropriate funeral ceremony practices, burial or cremation rites, ideas about appropriate dress, gifts, and flowers and suggestions for caring for the bereaved family during and after the funeral.

***Remembering Well: Rituals for Celebrating Life and Mourning Death*, by Sarah York; Jossey-Bass, 2000**

Offers practical guidelines for planning a service that involves the mourners and suits the unique context and person whose life is being remembered. Dozens of stories of individual rituals serve as examples of how a uniquely fitting memorial may be crafted.

***Saying Kaddish: How to Comfort the Dying, Bury the Dead, and Mourn as a Jew*, by Anita Diamant; Schocken, 1999**

Focuses on how Jews deal with the reality of death, from the sickroom until the end of the funeral, and explains the mitzvah of honoring the body.

***Transforming Rituals: Daily Practices for Changing Lives*, by Roy M. Oswald with Jean Morris Trumbauer; Alban Institute, 1999**

Explores rituals as spiritually healing practices for the home, congregation and broader community. Teaches congregational leaders how individuals and groups can use rituals to name, evaluate, live out, celebrate and grow through change.

Services for Grieving People

Some faith communities offer an annual service of remembrance for members who are experiencing grief. There are many possible service formats. Here is an outline for an order of worship that your congregation can use or customize with a prayer, music and scripture that fits your worship setting.

A. Gathering Music

B. Welcome

C. Words to Gather into Community

D. Prayer

E. Music

F. Scripture

G. A Brief Reflection or a
   Story of Remembrance

A clergy or layperson may lead a brief reflection on grief and remembrance, or a member may share his or her own journey with grief.

H. Lighting Candles

Place five unlit candles on a table or altar covered with a cloth. Lead a ritual of lighting candles as a way to support people in their grief. You may involve several people by asking them to do a reading or light one of the candles.

Here is an invocation and ritual you might use or adapt to fit with your faith community:

As we remember people we care about who have died, we turn our eyes to the powerful healing grief can bring. Together we light five symbolic candles: one of grief, one of joy, one of thanksgiving, one of community, one of love. These are reminders of the healing we seek.

1. We light this candle of grief to acknowledge the grief journey we travel. The journey may bring tears and anger and confusion and may cause us to question ourselves and God and to ask what life really means. Grief bursts in at the most

unexpected moments, times and places. Grief reminds us of the fullness of our relationship with the person who has died. And grief points us toward the healing that we seek.

2. We light this candle of joy as a sign that we knew joy with our loved one who has died. We celebrated together in life, and it is because we knew such joy that we now experience such sorrow. But because we knew joy first, we now know that even in our sorrow, our joy will come again. And it will come as we remember the life of the one we love.

3. We light this candle of thanksgiving in gratitude for the meaning this loved one brought into our lives, our families and our community. We are grateful as we remember, valuing what we learned and continue to learn, experienced and continue to experience, discovered and continue to discover, because of our loved one's life.

4. We light this candle of community to signify the community we create together in our remembering. Death has a way of sorting out what is most essential in life. Sometimes through our grief we see most clearly what really matters. And so we share that insight together in community, sharing with one another, seeking meaning together and supporting one another.

5. We light this final candle of love to honor our love of life and its mysterious but sure source. We honor our love for each other and for this world. We most especially honor our love for the one who has died and for the love hew or she shared with us. We honor the love that brings us together and sustains us all of our days. And we honor the love of God that assures us that even in our loneliest moments, we never walk alone.

May the light of these candles point us to the light we seek in our own lives. In the midst of our sorrow and grief, may we find healing and new life.

I. Lighting Individual Candles

J. Speaking Names

Distribute individual candles to participants when they arrive. At this point, use the fifth candle, above, to light one participant's candle and ask him or her to pass the light to a neighbor, inviting each to speak the name of the person being honored in the ceremony.

K. Responsive Reading or Poem

Read a responsive reading or poem, such as 'We Remember Them." (See below.)

L. Closing Words of Comfort

M. Music

SOURCE: DEVELOPED BY REV. JAMES BROOKS FOR BIG BEND HOSPICE IN TALLAHASSEE, FLORIDA

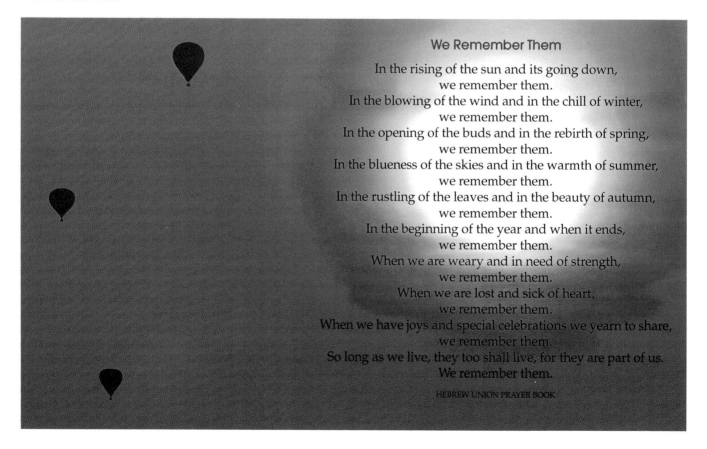

We Remember Them

In the rising of the sun and its going down,
we remember them.
In the blowing of the wind and in the chill of winter,
we remember them.
In the opening of the buds and in the rebirth of spring,
we remember them.
In the blueness of the skies and in the warmth of summer,
we remember them.
In the rustling of the leaves and in the beauty of autumn,
we remember them.
In the beginning of the year and when it ends,
we remember them.
When we are weary and in need of strength,
we remember them.
When we are lost and sick of heart,
we remember them.
When we have joys and special celebrations we yearn to share,
we remember them.
So long as we live, they too shall live, for they are part of us.
We remember them.

HEBREW UNION PRAYER BOOK

Services Recognizing Grief

Some faith traditions and communities incorporate services of remembrance into special services during the year.

For example, in Jewish tradition, mourning is fully integrated into worship through the public observance of the kaddish and through special services during the year.

- Yizkor. This memorial service, the public observance for the community of bereaved, is recited four times a year during holiday services following the reading of the Torah. Jewish holidays include two in the fall: Yom Kippur and the Shemini Atzeret and two in the spring: the eighth day of Passover and the Shavuot. Of these holidays, Yom Kippur and Passover are observed most often.

- Yom Hashoah. Also known as Holocaust Remembrance Day, this holiday falls at different times on the secular calendar each year.

Christian tradition has some special seasons or holiday observances when grief support can be a fit.

- All Saints Day. One remembrance connected with All Saints Day, on November 1, is called Totenfest. This annual ritual originated in the German Evangelical tradition of the United Church of Christ. Family members of people who have died during the year are invited to come forward as family representative or acolyte lights a candle for each person being remembered. Flowers may be presented to family members, and people in the congregation may be invited to add additional names of people they are remembering. (For more information about Totenfest, go to www. ucc.org/assets/pdfs/totenfest.pdf.)

- Blue Christmas or Longest Night Service. This worship service specifically addresses holiday sadness. Blue Christmas seeks to assure people that feeling sorrow during the holidays is understandable and acceptable even though others are joyous. These services typically take place on or near December 21, which is the longest night of the year. However, they may be offered any time during advent. (For more on this, go to www.gbod.org/worship/default.asp?act=reader&item_id=5630&loc_id=9,612,636.)

- Good Friday. A Good Friday service, held the Friday before Easter, may include discordant music, a litany of complaint, time for silence, hymns of lament, a call for cries of abandonment, a witness to the story of Christ's death and a dismissal that echoes cries of loss rather than hope. One model, "A Service of Silence and Lamentation for Good Friday or Holy Saturday" can be found in the appendix of *Journey Through the Psalms*, by Denise Dombkowski Hopkins; Christian Board of Publication, 2006.

- Memorial Day. Some congregations invite family members of people who have died during the previous year to come to a Memorial Day worship service that includes a time of remembrance. One ritual some congregations enact is creating a bouquet of flowers. An empty vase in placed in a prominent place before the service. The names of people who have died are then read aloud. Family members come forward with a rose given to them by a representative of the congregation. Family members place a rose in the vase, adding to the growing arrangement, or hand the rose to a congregation member, who adds the rose to the vase. By the end of the ritual, the individual flowers have become a bouquet—a reminder that the people who have died are individuals who are also part of a community.

Kaddish in Worship

In Jewish tradition, the kaddish, Aramaic for "holy," is a prayer that expresses praise and glorification of God and the hope for the creation of God's kingdom on earth. The mourners' kaddish may be said every day for 11 months after the death of a parent, spouse, child or sibling—and subsequently on each anniversary of the death, called yahrzeit.

As part of worship, the mourners' kaddish is recited at the end of the synagogue service. Kaddish is recited standing, facing Jerusalem. In some communities, the entire congregation stands; in others, only the mourners.

The Kaddish

Magnified and sanctified is God's great name throughout the world which God created. Speedily may God's kingship reign for all our days, during our lifetime and the lifetimes of all the people of Israel. Let us say: Amen.

May God's great name be blessed throughout eternity.

Blessed, honored, glorified, exalted, extolled, decorated, lauded and praised is God's holy name beyond all blessing, song and tribute that we may ever offer. Let us say: Amen.

May great peace descend from the heavens along with the full life upon us and upon all Israel. Let us say: Amen.

May the One who makes peace in the universe grant peace to us and to all Israel. Let us say: Amen.

SOURCE: *JEWISH RITUAL,REALITY AND RESPONSE AT THE END OF LIFE: A GUIDE TO CARING FOR JEWISH PATIENTS AND THEIR FAMILIES*, DUKE INSTITUTE ON CARE AT THE END OF LIFE, 2007

Creative Rituals for Grief Support

As discussed in the chapter titled Creating Unbroken Circles of Care, there are creative ways congregations can adapt their spaces to offer support during times of illness, end of life and grief. A few of those specifically aimed at grief are outlined below.

A Robe of Remembrance

Creating a Robe of Remembrance is a powerful and artistic way to honor individuals who have died. Using a simple robe, congregations invite members to pick a button that reminds them in some way of the person they are remembering or to select a button from that person's clothing. Then they are invited to sew a button on the robe in that person's memory. As an additional step, they may record a story about the button, including their memories, in a book of remembrance that accompanies the robe. The robe can hang in a designated location and members may add buttons over time.

Project Compassion offers instructions for creating a Robe of Remembrance along with templates and examples at www.project-compassion.org.

Virtual Places

Virtual places of remembrance allow faith communities to create Internet-based places for remembering without changing their existing space. One example of a free virtual remembering space is "We Remember Them" at www.we-remember-them.com. Funeral homes and newspapers have also developed virtual places for remembrance that can service as models. Congregations can refer members to existing resources or create one of their own using existing sites as models.

Permanent Places

Many faith communities traditionally had cemeteries adjacent to their property. While some congregations still maintain this tradition, operating a cemetery is no longer an option for many. Congregations that do have cemeteries may benefit from adding new spaces for remembering to existing memorial spaces.

Creating a permanent place for remembering is a way to designate sacred space for remembering on congregational property. There are a number of options to consider.

A Remembering Garden offers a place for people to experience nature as they deal with their grief. It can include plantings, walkways, benches and possibly a structure, such as a gazebo. While a remembering garden does not hold the remains of people who have died, the garden may have a plaque, book or memorial artwork for remembering members.

A Memorial Garden provides a place for congregations that do not have a cemetery to bury or sprinkle member's ashes on congregational grounds. Congregations creating a memorial garden are wise to create a policy regarding the garden specifying who may be buried there, the type of containers allowed for ashes—often only bio-degradable containers—and where and how names of people buried there will be included. It will be important to think ahead, anticipating how many names may be added in the coming 25 years.

A Remembrance Walk is a pathway for remembering people who have died. The path is often paved with bricks engraved with the names of people being remembered. Bricks are often added annually or semi-annually. A walk can be constructed on its own or incorporated into a Memorial Garden.

In creating a place for remembering, consider questions such as:

- What space will you designate for this purpose?

- Will you establish a consistent design and look?

- Will your space for remembering be fully accessible for people in wheelchairs and with limited mobility?

- If you use bricks or markers, will you include only names only or will you also or include dates, symbols?

- Who will supply the bricks or markers?

- How often will you add bricks or add names to a marker?

- What will be the cost?

- Will you create a fund for people who cannot afford the cost?

- How will you maintain your place for remembering?

- Will you use your place for remembering for other purposes as well, such as weddings, musical concerts or remembrance services?

Establishing a permanent place for remembering is a way to involve the congregation in tending a garden as part of remembering life. Such as place for remembering can become a way to honor all the seasons of life through the seasons of the year.

W e ask for a generous spirit and tolerance concerning language and semantics. Because this toolkit is intended for a diverse audience of readers, it uses a specific vocabulary of spiritual and religious language aimed to communicate across congregational settings, as set out in this glossary. However, because all language has limitations, you may need to make some adjustments in your setting and tradition.

Clergy: Religious officials or functionaries—such as ministers, pastors, priests and rabbis—who are prepared and authorized to conduct religious services or attend to other religious duties.

Congregation: A gathering or assembly of people that meets for worship and for religious instruction. Also applies to interfaith groups.

Denomination: A defined religious body within a larger faith tradition that uses a common name, structure or doctrine. For example, The United Methodist Church is a denomination in the Christian faith tradition.

Faith community: A group of individuals joined by common beliefs and forms of worship.

Faith community nurse: A professional nurse, as defined by local and state licensing regulations, who serves on the staff of a congregation to promote health issues for its members and the community. Also known as a parish nurse, congregational nurse, crescent nurse or health ministry nurse.

Faith tradition: A set of beliefs centered upon specific spiritual beliefs and moral teachings—and often organized, defined or codified through scripture, prayer, ritual and religious law. May also incorporate ancestral histories or cultural traditions. Christianity, Judiasm, Islam and Buddhism are examples of some major faith traditions.

God: Refers to the supreme being or a higher power, recognizing that each person and faith tradition applies a unique meaning and understanding.

Interdenominational: Occurring between or among different churches or denominations within the same religious tradition, such as a partnership between Presbyterians and Methodists.

Interfaith: Occurring between or among people or organizations of different faiths or traditions, such as a Christian-Jewish-Moslem dialogue or partnership.

Lay leader: Member of a faith community who does not function as clergy, but takes on a voluntary leadership role within a congregation.

Member: Individual who belongs to a faith community. Also commonly called a congregant or parishioner.

Ministry: Activity or service of a faith community that supports others.

Religion: A set of beliefs and practices organized, defined or codified through prayer, ritual, religious law or teaching.

Spiritual: Relating to sacred or religious matters—usually with the common thread of connecting to God, a higher power, others, the self or the earth.

To provide feedback on this toolkit, go to **www.iceol.duke.edu.**

*Will the circle
be unbroken?
By and by, Lord, by and by.
There's a better life awaiting
If we try, Lord, if we try.*

Traditional folk song
arranged by A.P. Carter